Words to Learn By

EXPANDING Academic Vocabulary

Stephen Dolainski • S. Elizabeth Griffin

D1220661

McGraw Hill **Education**

Bothell, WA • Chicago, IL • Columbus, OH • New York, NY

Authors: Stephen Dolainski and Elizabeth Griffin

Stephen Dolainski is an adult educator, editor, and author. He has worked with the Los Angeles Unified School District for 18 years. As the Adult Basic Education Program adviser, Stephen supports teachers in classrooms across the district. He participated in the federal STAR initiative in California, and he completed training in evidence-based adult reading instruction. Now he trains other teachers to use evidence-based instruction in their classrooms. As an instructor, he has taught English as a Second Language (ESL), Adult Secondary Education, and Adult Basic Education (ABE). He is the author of *Grammar Traps: A Handbook of the 20 Most Common Grammar Mistakes and How to Avoid Them,* and he has contributed to numerous publications.

S. Elizabeth Griffin is an adult educator and teacher trainer. She has worked with a wide variety of students in a number of different programs from Peace Corps to Refugee Projects to Community Adult Schools. For almost 30 years, she has worked with students and teachers in the Los Angeles area. As an Adult Basic Education adviser for Los Angeles Unified School District, she participated in the federal STAR initiative in California and attended STAR trainings to deliver evidence-based adult reading instruction. She has trained adult education teachers and parole program teachers in evidence-based reading instruction. During her career, she has taught ESL, ABE, and Adult High-School-GED students. She currently works as a private consultant and trainer.

www.mheonline.com

 **Education**

Send all inquiries to:
Contemporary/McGraw-Hill
130 East Randolph Street, Suite 400
Chicago, IL 60601

ISBN   978-0-07-658633-2
MHID   0-07-658633-2

3 4 5 6 7 8 9 QDB 15 14 13 12 11

Contents

To the Student

Vocabulary is a key that unlocks meaning and comprehension. It opens doors to new ideas. It helps you become a better reader, writer, and student.

In *Words to Learn By: Expanding Academic Vocabulary* you will learn 100 words. These words were carefully chosen for you. They are high-frequency academic words. What does high-frequency mean? It means you will find these words everywhere.

You will find them in textbooks and in reference books and on tests. You will also find these words in magazines, newspapers, and work-related materials. You will hear them in conversations at school or work, and on radio and television.

By learning these words, you will become a more successful student. These words will help you no matter what you are reading. They will also help you in classroom discussions and in your writing.

How to Use the Book

Words to Learn By: Expanding Academic Vocabulary has five units. Each unit includes four lessons. In each lesson you will learn five high-frequency words. First, the teacher will explain the meaning of each word and give examples. Then you will practice using the words.

It is important to use these words when you are not in class. Use them when you talk to friends and people at work. Listen for the words in conversations and on radio and television. If you are a parent, use the words with your children.

We believe that *Words to Learn By: Expanding Academic Vocabulary* will help you reach your academic goals. We wish you much success!

Stephen Dolainski and Elizabeth Griffin

consequence

phase

appropriate

basis

rely

consistent

determine

content

symbol

recognize

circumstance

appear

outcome

critical

sufficient

although

represent

challenge

express

emphasize

appropriate basis circumstance appear
although rely **content** critical challenge
recognize consequence emphasize phase
express outcome consistent **represent**
critical sufficient **symbol** determine rely

Vocabulary Knowledge Rating Chart

How well do you know the words? Use the numbers to rate your knowledge of the vocabulary words. Follow the teacher's directions.

4 = I know the word. I know it well enough to teach it to someone else.
3 = The word is familiar. I think I know what it means.
2 = I have heard the word, but I'm not sure what it means.
1 = I don't know the word at all.

	My rating before instruction	I think the word means	My rating after instruction
appropriate			
content			
recognize			
represent			
symbol			

Word Meaning Chart

Complete the chart. Follow the teacher's directions.

appropriate *(adjective)* /uh PROH pree eyt/
The word **appropriate** describes something that is right or acceptable.

EXAMPLES

A bouquet of flowers is an _____ gift for someone in the hospital.

Class Example: _____

My Example: It is **appropriate** to wear _____ to school.

content *(noun)* /KON tent/
Content means the items, information, or ideas that are in something.

EXAMPLES

The _____ of the speech was mainly political.

Class Example: _____

My Example: I can list the **contents** of my _____

recognize *(verb)* /REK uhg nahyz/
To **recognize** means to know someone or something from the past, or to know that an idea is true or important.

EXAMPLES

A good teacher _____ that all students learn differently.

Class Example: _____

My Example: I did not **recognize** my friend because _____

represent *(verb)* /re pri ZENT/
To **represent** means to stand for someone or something.

EXAMPLES

The stripes on the American flag _____ the thirteen original colonies.

Class Example: _____

My Example: One person who **represents** my state in Congress is _____

symbol *(noun)* /SIM buhl/
A **symbol** identifies an idea, feeling, or place.

EXAMPLES

The dove is a _____ of peace.

Class Example: _____

My Example: A **symbol** of graduation is _____

Exercise 1   Use the Words

Complete each sentence. Write the correct form of the vocabulary word in the blank space.

1. In the television interview, the governor _____ that the economy was improving.

2. International signs and _____ help travelers around the world.

3. The library is an _____ place to study.

4. How many athletes _____ the United States in the last Olympic Games?

5. The _____ of the insurance policy were not very clear to me.

Exercise 2   Complete the Sentences

These sentences have been started for you. They are not complete. Complete them with your own words.

1. The contents of Uncle Frank's letter surprised everyone because _____

   _____

   _____

2. Two symbols of America are _____

   _____

   _____

3. I recognize that someone needs help when _____

   _____

   _____

   _____

4. To me a high school diploma represents _____

   _____

   _____

5. The movie is not appropriate for young children because _____

   _____

   _____

Words at Work

Circle the best answer to each multiple choice question below. Then write a brief response to the question that follows. Write your answers in complete sentences.

1. During the orientation, Mr. Lee told the new employees that it is essential for them to dress professionally, be polite, and speak clearly. Why is this important?

   (A) They represent the company to the customers.
   (B) They represent the customers to the company.
   (C) They represent the company to their supervisors.

   When have you represented your school, work, or family? _____

   _____

   _____

2. Miles had car problems, so his coworker Amy gave him rides to work for several days. Miles wants to thank Amy. What is an appropriate way for Miles to thank Amy?

   (A) write a letter to the boss about Amy
   (B) say nothing because this is a workplace
   (C) buy lunch for Amy and say thank you

   What is another appropriate way to thank a coworker? _____

   _____

   _____

3. The owners of Sully's Seafood Heaven are looking for a new symbol to put on the sign and the menu. What would make an appropriate symbol?

   (A) a star and a rainbow
   (B) a heart and a star
   (C) a fish and a star

   What is a business or company you know that has a symbol? What does the symbol

   represent? _____

   _____

   _____

4. Marta recognized that the young child she was babysitting was very tired. How did Marta recognize that?

   (A) The child rubbed her eyes and cried.
   (B) The child sat down and played with her toys.
   (C) The child took off her shoes and sat down.

   How do you recognize when someone you work with is tired? What do you do? _____

   _____

   _____

Exercise 4 Word Families

Most words are part of a family of words. Study the word families on this page. Then fill in the missing words in the sentences below using the words from this lesson. Use the correct form of each word to complete the sentences.

---

appropriate *(adjective)*

- appropriately *(adverb)*
  Be on time and dress appropriately for the interview.

recognize *(verb)*

- recognition *(noun)*
  The recognition of a problem leads to a solution.

content *(noun)*

- contain *(verb)*
  The box contains cookies and candy for the class.
- table of contents *(noun)*
  The table of contents is in the front of a book and tells how the book is organized.

represent *(verb)*

- representative *(noun)*
  The union representative scheduled a meeting before work.
- representative *(adjective)*
  The clerk's unpleasant attitude is not representative of the store's service.

symbol *(noun)*

- symbolic *(adjective)*
  The disabled veteran completed the race. It was a symbolic victory for him.
- symbolize *(verb)*
  Wedding rings symbolize the promise to be faithful.

---

1. The donkey is a _____ of the Democrats, and the elephant

_____ the Republicans.

2. Did Mr. Nunez meet with the sales _____ from the printing company?

3. Mrs. Chung was pleased when her son behaved _____ at the wedding.

4. Does this tea _____ caffeine?

5. The _____ of the need for space exploration grew in the 1950s.

Reading a Textbook

It is important to _____ the different parts of a textbook. The
                          6.

_____ is found at the front of the book. It lists the _____
        7.   **8.**

of the book by chapter, lesson, or unit number. The glossary _____
                                                                      9.

important words and their meanings. Some textbooks use _____ such
                                                                10.

as a pencil to _____ a writing activity.
                    11.

Is success easy to recognize?

Exercise 5 What Do You Think?

Read each question and write a brief answer. Explain your answers in complete sentences.

1. Is money always a symbol of a successful life? Do a beautiful home and expensive cars represent success? What symbolizes success?

_____

_____

_____

2. Is it ever appropriate for parents to read the contents of a child's email?

_____

_____

_____

3. Is it appropriate for a teacher to publicly recognize students' feelings and attitudes?

_____

_____

_____

Reading Connection

Read the following passage and answer the questions.

The Space Race to the Moon

On July 16, 1969, three American astronauts left planet Earth in a spacecraft called Apollo 11. The astronauts were Neil Armstrong, Buzz Aldrin, and Michael Collins. They were headed for the moon, 239,000 miles away. Four days later, Apollo 11 reached the moon. The astronauts put Apollo 11 into an orbit to circle the moon.

Apollo 11 had two parts. They were named *Columbia* and *Eagle*. The *Columbia* was the main part. It was the command module. Astronaut Collins stayed on the *Columbia*. Astronauts Armstrong and Aldrin descended to the surface of the moon in the *Eagle*.

The astronauts had a television camera to record the event. People around the world watched as Neil Armstrong became the first human being to step onto the moon. As he did it, he said, "That's one small step for man, one giant leap for mankind." Buzz Aldrin joined Neil Armstrong on the moon's surface.

Astronauts Aldrin and Armstrong spent two hours exploring the moon's surface. They collected rock and soil samples. They did science experiments, took photographs, and put up an American flag. Later the *Eagle* returned to the *Columbia* for the journey home to Earth. The astronauts splashed down in the Pacific Ocean on July 24, 1969.

Between 1969 and 1972, five more Apollo spacecraft took astronauts to the moon. The moon landings ended in December 1972 with Apollo 17.

The purpose of sending astronauts to the moon was mainly political. In those days, the United States and the former Soviet Union were fighting a "cold war." Each country tried to show it was stronger and smarter than the other country. One way to do that was to win a "space race" to send astronauts to the moon. The United States won the Space Race, but the Cold War continued for two more decades.

1. When Apollo 11 returned to Earth, what contents from the moon did the astronauts bring back?

_____

_____

2. What did the moon landing represent to the United States?

_____

_____

3. Why was Neil Armstrong's statement an appropriate response to being the first person on the moon? What did he represent when he stepped onto the moon?

_____

_____

appropriate basis circumstance appear
although rely **content** critical challenge
recognize consequence emphasize phase
express outcome consistent **represent**
critical sufficient **symbol** determine rely

New Word List

☐ appropriate

☐ content

☐ recognize

☐ represent

☐ symbol

Writing Connection

Write a brief response to each question. Use words from this lesson in your answer. Write your answers in complete sentences.

What does becoming a citizen of the U.S. represent to most immigrants? Why is it important to them? Give at least two examples.

_____

_____

_____

_____

_____

In a family, it is important to recognize the needs of each individual family member. How can parents recognize the individual needs of their children? Explain your answer with examples.

_____

_____

_____

_____

_____

_____

_____

Exercise 8 Reflection

Think about the words you have studied in this lesson.

1. Which words did you enjoy learning? _____

2. Select one word and imagine where you will use the word. Explain the situation.

_____

_____

3. Which words do you still need help with? _____

4. Return to the Knowledge Rating Chart at the beginning of this lesson. Complete column 3. How have your responses changed?

appropriate **although** circumstance appear
basis rely emphasize critical challenge
recognize **consequence** phase express
appear outcome represent **consistent**
critical phase symbol **determine** content

Vocabulary Knowledge Rating Chart

How well do you know the words? Use the numbers to rate your knowledge of the vocabulary words. Follow the teacher's directions.

4 = I know the word. I know it well enough to teach it to someone else.
3 = The word is familiar. I think I know what it means.
2 = I have heard the word, but I'm not sure what it means.
1 = I don't know the word at all.

	My rating before instruction	I think the word means	My rating after instruction
although			
basis			
consequence			
consistent			
determine			

Word Meaning Chart

Complete the chart. Follow the teacher's directions.

although *(conjunction)* /awl THOH/
The word **although** is used to show contrast between two ideas in the same sentence.

EXAMPLES

Jake was not chosen for the basketball team _____ he played well.

Class Example: _____

My Example: **Although** I was tired, I _____

basis *(noun)* /BEY sis/
Basis means the main reason or idea for doing or organizing something.

EXAMPLES

The sinking of the *Titanic* has been the _____ of several movies.

Class Example: _____

My Example: Something I do on a weekly **basis** is _____

consequence *(noun)* /KON si kwens/
Consequence means the result, usually negative, of an action or situation.

EXAMPLES

A speeding ticket is a _____ of driving too fast.

Class Example: _____

My Example: A **consequence** of not studying is _____

consistent *(adjective)* /kuhn SIS tuhnt/
Consistent means that something or someone continues to act or be the same.

EXAMPLES

The warm weather was _____ for a week until it rained today.

Class Example: _____

My Example: **Consistent** attendance at school is important because _____

determine *(verb)* /dih TUR min/
To **determine** means to figure out, solve, or decide something.

EXAMPLES

Teachers _____ students' grades.

Class Example: _____

My Example: Using a map, we **determined** _____

Exercise 1 Use the Words

Complete each sentence. Write the correct form of the vocabulary word in the blank space.

1. An oil spill in the ocean has serious _____ for people and sea life.

2. Many pioneers chose to travel west in covered wagons _____ the trip was difficult and dangerous.

3. Discipline for children is effective if it is _____ .

4. A jury considers the evidence to _____ if a person is guilty or not.

5. Rice is the _____ of many Asian diets.

Exercise 2 Complete the Sentences

These sentences have been started for you. They are not complete. Complete them with your own words.

1. Miranda goes to school on a part-time basis because _____

   _____

   _____

2. Mrs. Medina read her recipe for pecan pie and

   determined _____

   _____

   _____

3. Although the apartment was old, it _____

   _____

   _____

4. My consistent morning routine includes _____

   _____

   _____

5. As a consequence of lying to his mother, Maurice _____

   _____

   _____

Words at Work

Circle the best answer to each multiple choice question below. Then write a brief response to the question that follows. Write your answers in complete sentences.

1. Lindsay's manager told her that she needs to be more consistent in her work. What did her manager mean?

   (A) Lindsay always does good work.
   (B) Lindsay never does good work.
   (C) Lindsay sometimes does good work.

   Why is a consistent job performance important?_____

   _____

   _____

2. Regis determined that he cannot afford to buy a new car right now. What was something he considered to determine this?

   (A) the color of the car
   (B) the kind of car his teacher drives
   (C) the cost of insurance for the new car

   What is something you determined you could or could not afford to buy? What did you consider?

   _____

   _____

   _____

3. Rolando interviewed two people for one hotel job. Now he must determine which person to hire. What should be the basis for his decision?

   (A) the person's gender
   (B) the person's experience
   (C) the person's age

   What other things could be used as the basis for hiring someone? _____

   _____

   _____

4. Mindy got a parking ticket and forgot to pay it on time. What was the consequence?

   (A) The fine was increased.
   (B) She got another ticket.
   (C) She lost her license.

   What is a consequence you experienced because you were late for something? _____

   _____

   _____

   _____

Exercise 4 Word Families

Most words are part of a family of words. Study the word families on this page. Then fill in the missing words in the sentences below using the words from this lesson. Use the correct form of each word to complete the sentences.

---

although *(conjunction)*

- even though *(conjunction)*
  Randy went to work today even though he did not feel well.

- though *(conjunction)*
  The twins have very different personalities though they look alike.

basis *(noun)*

- based on *(verb)*
  What information was your decision based on?

- basic *(adjective)*
  It is helpful to have a basic understanding of how computers work.

consequence *(noun)*

- consequently *(adverb)*
  The storm caused the power to go out. Consequently, the lights did not work.

consistent *(adjective)*

- consistently *(adverb)*
  Raquel consistently remembers every coworker's birthday.

- consistency *(noun)*
  The consistency of the team's skills helped them win the game.

---

1. The painting of the cathedral was _____ a photograph taken in Paris.

2. The chart demonstrated that the company's sales increased _____ each month for the last year.

3. Elizabeth left her wallet at home. _____, she did not have enough money to buy lunch.

4. Did the orientation session answer the _____ questions you had?

5. We like this restaurant because of the _____ in the quality of the food.

6. _____ *The Wonderful Wizard of Oz* was written more than 100 years ago, the book is still popular.

Reading Aloud to Children

_____ the research, children benefit when their parents
<small>7.</small>

_____ read aloud to them. _____ young children
<small>8.</small> <small>9.</small>

don't understand all the words, they enjoy hearing their parents' voices. They also enjoy looking

at books with pictures. They learn to recognize words on the page. _____,
<small>10.</small>

they are better prepared for reading in school.

What is the secret to living a long life?

Exercise 5 What Do You Think?

Read each question and write a brief answer. Explain your answers in complete sentences.

1. Is longevity, or living a long life, determined more on the basis of family history (genetics) or lifestyle choices?

   _____

   _____

   _____

2. Is consistent practice more important in determining success for a musician or for an athlete?

   _____

   _____

   _____

3. Are there consequences for society if men and women are not treated on an equal basis?

   _____

   _____

   _____

Reading Connection

Read the following passage and answer the questions.

Supreme Court Justice Sonia Sotomayor

Sonia Sotomayor made history on August 6, 2009. That day she became the first Hispanic justice on the United States Supreme Court. She also became the third woman to serve on the court in its 220-year history.

Sonia Sotomayor was born in 1954 in the Bronx, a section of New York City. Her parents moved to New York from Puerto Rico. Sonia's father, Juan, was a tool and die worker. He did not speak English. He died when Sonia was nine years old. Sonia's mother, Celina, worked as a nurse. She raised Sonia and Sonia's brother, Juan, as a single mother after her husband died. Celina sent her two children to private Catholic schools.

The family lived close to Yankee Stadium, and Sonia became a fan of the New York Yankees baseball team. As a young girl, Sonia wanted to become a detective. She changed her mind after watching *Perry Mason*, a television show about a lawyer. She decided to become a judge.

Sonia was at the head of her high school class. She went to college at Princeton University. At that time, there were few Hispanic students at Princeton. Although the work at Princeton was challenging at first for Sonia, she worked hard and graduated with honors. Then she attended Yale Law School. "I was raised in a Bronx public housing project, but studied at two of the nation's finest universities," she says.

Sonia worked in New York City as a district attorney and as a lawyer in private practice. She became a federal judge in 1991. In 2009, President Obama nominated her for the Supreme Court.

Sonia Sotomayor knows that many people helped her become part of history. However, she says, "There is one extraordinary person who is my life aspiration. That person is my mother, Celina Sotomayor."

1. On what basis did Sonia Sotomayor become part of American history?

_____

_____

2. Although Sonia Sotomayor struggled at first with the work at Princeton, she graduated with honors. What does this tell us about the kind of person she is?

_____

_____

3. Do you think Celina Sotomayor was a consistent role model for her daughter? Why?

_____

_____

_____

approximate **although** circumstance appear
basis rely emphasize critical challenge
recognize **consequence** phase express
appear outcome represent **consistent**
critical phase symbol **determine** content

New Word List

☐ although

☐ basis

☐ consequence

☐ consistent

☐ determine

Review Word List

☐ _____

☐ _____

☐ _____

☐ _____

☐ _____

Writing Connection

Write a brief response to each question. Use words from this lesson or the previous lesson in your answer. Write your answers in complete sentences.

Confucius is one of China's most famous teachers and philosophers. He once said, "When anger rises, think of the consequences." What did he mean?

_____

_____

_____

_____

_____

Think about an important decision you made recently. What was the basis for your decision? Were there any consequences?

_____

_____

_____

_____

_____

Reflection

Think about the words you have studied in this lesson.

1. Which words did you enjoy learning? _____

2. Select one word and imagine where you will use the word. Explain the situation.

_____

_____

3. Which words do you still need help with? _____

4. Return to the Knowledge Rating Chart at the beginning of this lesson. Complete column 3. How have your responses changed?

circumstance appear critical although
basis determine content **critical** appropriate
recognize consequence emphasize **express**
phase appear outcome represent consistent
symbol sufficient **rely** appropriate determine

Vocabulary Knowledge Rating Chart

How well do you know the words? Use the numbers to rate your knowledge of the vocabulary words. Follow the teacher's directions.

4 = I know the word. I know it well enough to teach it to someone else.
3 = The word is familiar. I think I know what it means.
2 = I have heard the word, but I'm not sure what it means.
1 = I don't know the word at all.

	My rating before instruction	I think the word means	My rating after instruction
circumstance			
critical			
express			
phase			
rely			

Word Meaning Chart

Complete the chart. Follow the teacher's directions.

circumstance *(noun)* /SUR kuhm stans/
A circumstance is a condition or detail concerning an event or situation.

EXAMPLES

How often students can come to night class depends on their _____.

Class Example: _____

My Example: The **circumstances** of my life permit me to _____

critical *(adjective)* /KRIT i kuhl/
The word **critical** describes something that is very important and serious.

EXAMPLES

It is _____ for firefighters to respond quickly to emergency calls.

Class Example: _____

My Example: A **critical** issue for our country at the moment is _____

express *(verb)* /ik SPRES/
To **express** is to tell or show thoughts and feelings with words, actions, or looks.

EXAMPLES

Richard gave his neighbor a box of candy to _____ his thanks for taking care of his dog.

Class Example: _____

My Example: I often **express** an opinion about _____

phase *(noun)* /feyz/
Phase means a step or stage in a process.

EXAMPLES

During the penalty _____ of a trial, the jury determines the punishment.

Class Example: _____

My Example: The first **phase** of a project is usually for _____

rely *(verb)* /ri LAHY/
To **rely** on something or someone means to depend on or trust them.

EXAMPLES

Students _____ on teachers to prepare them for tests and exams.

Class Example: _____

My Example: People **rely** on their computers to _____

Exercise 1   Use the Words

Complete each sentence. Write the correct form of the vocabulary word in the blank space.

1. "The next game is _____," the coach told the team. "If we lose, we are out of the tournament."

2. The committee is in the second _____ of the investigation. They are reading and reviewing all available information.

3. Under normal _____, I can work on weekends, but my sister is getting married this Saturday.

4. People in the 19th century _____ on telegrams to communicate important news and information.

5. Did the community group meet with the mayor to _____ its opposition to the planned high-rise buildings?

Exercise 2   Complete the Sentences

These sentences have been started for you. They are not complete. Complete them with your own words.

1. A project with several phases that I worked on was _____

   _____

   _____

2. A critical decision I will have to make is _____

   _____

   _____

3. I can't rely on _____ because _____

   _____

   _____

4. Tony and I are in similar circumstances because _____

   _____

   _____

5. Sometimes it is difficult for me to express myself when _____

   _____

   _____

Words at Work

Circle the best answer to each multiple choice question below. Then write a brief response to the question that follows. Write your answers in complete sentences.

1. Mark is taking a four-week training course, which he finds very interesting and useful. He is in the final phase of the training. What is Mark doing now?

   (A) He is practicing what he has learned.

   (B) He is learning new methods.

   (C) He is learning which tools to use.

   What would usually happen in the first phase of training? _____

   _____

   _____

2. Gloria spoke to her manager and expressed an interest in working the afternoon shift. What did she say?

   (A) "I can't work the afternoon shift."

   (B) "I would like to work the afternoon shift."

   (C) "The afternoon shift is the most popular shift."

   When did you last express an interest in doing something at school or work? _____

   _____

   _____

3. Glenda had an accident at work. She fell and hurt her back, so she had to fill out an accident report form. One of the questions on the form asked her to describe the circumstances of the accident. What did Glenda include in her answer?

   (A) She was wearing blue jeans.

   (B) The windows were open.

   (C) The floor was wet.

   Why is it important to know the circumstances of an accident? _____

   _____

   _____

4. Mr. Lopez recognizes that he relies on one of his workers, Bob, more than the others. What indicates that Mr. Lopez relies on Bob?

   (A) Mr. Lopez always asks Bob to train new workers.

   (B) Mr. Lopez and Bob have a similar interest in basketball.

   (C) Mr. Lopez reminds Bob to punch his time card.

   Name a person you rely on at work or school. Explain why you rely on that person. _____

   _____

   _____

Word Families

Most words are part of a family of words. Study the word families on this page. Then fill in the missing words in the sentences below using the words from this lesson. Use the correct form of each word to complete the sentences.

---

critical *(adjective)*

- **critically** *(adverb)*
  The critically injured people were taken to the hospital immediately.

express *(verb)*

- **expression** *(noun)*
  Freedom of expression is one of the most important rights Americans have.

rely *(verb)*

- **reliable** *(adjective)*
  Maggie is a reliable babysitter. She is always on time.

- **reliance** *(noun)*
  Every political candidate promises to reduce America's reliance on foreign oil.

- **reliant** *(adjective)*
  The ambassador was reliant on her staff to make appointments.

- **self-reliance** *(noun)*
  The American cowboy is well known for his independence and self-reliance.

---

1. Our _____ on cell phones increases each year.

2. The runner's facial _____ indicated he was struggling to finish the race.

3. The car is old but it is _____. It takes me where I need to go.

4. Habitat for Humanity _____ on donations to operate.

5. Medicine and other supplies were _____ needed after the earthquake.

6. Jose's _____ was one reason he was successful.

Cars

America's _____ on the car increased in the second half of the 20th
                    7.
century. Before the 1950s, people _____ on trains and streetcars. This
                                  8.
was a critical change. As more people _____ their need for cars, more car
                                      9.
factories were built. Modern highways were also _____ needed. The
                                                10.
car became a symbol of _____ and an _____
                       11.   **12.**
of independence.

Winning the lottery can change your life.

Exercise 5 What Do You Think?

Read each question and write a brief answer. Explain your answers in complete sentences.

1. If you won the lottery, how would your circumstances change? Could you rely on family and friends in the same way you did before winning the lottery?

   _____

   _____

   _____

2. Which phase of a person's career is the most critical—the beginning, middle, or end?

   _____

   _____

   _____

3. Is it appropriate for a doctor to express an opinion about the circumstances of a patient's lifestyle?

   _____

   _____

   _____

Reading Connection

Read the following passage and answer the questions.

The Great Wall of China

More than 2,000 years ago, China was made up of many tribes of different groups of people. There was fighting between the tribes. To protect themselves, some of the tribes built walls around sections of land they controlled. Qin Shi Huang became the first emperor of China when he united many of the tribes to form one state. To protect his empire from invaders from the north, he ordered the construction of a new wall. The new wall joined together sections of the old walls the tribes had built.

It took 300,000 workers to build the new wall. The wall stretched for thousands of miles across northern China. It went through mountains, valleys, forests, and fields. It was difficult to transport building materials, so the builders used local materials when possible. In the mountains, they constructed the wall with rocks and stones. In the flat plains, they used earth to build it. Centuries later, bricks were used to rebuild or to add new sections to the wall.

The Great Wall was 3,800 miles long. In some places it was 25 feet high and 19 feet wide. It was wide enough on top for several people to stand next to each other. It was the largest military structure in the world. It was successful in keeping out invaders until around 1600 when the Manchus, a tribe from the north, crossed the wall.

The wall has become known as the Great Wall of China. Through the years, much of it has collapsed. People took the stones to build houses. Portions that were made of earth have eroded away. However, large sections of it remain standing, and millions of people visit the Great Wall each year.

Today, the Great Wall of China is recognized as an important historical structure and has been put on the list of World Heritage sites.

1. What were the circumstances that led to the construction of the Great Wall of China?

_____

_____

2. Does China rely on the Great Wall today in the same way it did 2,000 years ago?

_____

_____

3. Explain the phases the Great Wall has gone through in its history.

_____

_____

circumstance appear critical although
basis determine content **critical** appropriate
recognize consequence emphasize **express**
phase appear outcome represent consistent
symbol sufficient **rely** appropriate determine

New Word List

☐ circumstance

☐ critical

☐ express

☐ phase

☐ rely

Review Word List

☐ _____

☐ _____

☐ _____

☐ _____

☐ _____

Exercise 7 Writing Connection

Write a brief response to each question. Use words from this lesson or previous lessons in your answer. Write your answers in complete sentences.

Reflect on a time when the circumstances of an event or situation changed for you or your family. What happened? What were the consequences?

_____

_____

_____

_____

Is it always wise to express your feelings? Use specific examples to explain your answer.

_____

_____

_____

_____

Exercise 8 Reflection

Think about the words you have studied in this lesson.

1. Which words did you enjoy learning? _____

2. Select one word and imagine where you will use the word. Explain the situation.

_____

_____

3. Which words do you still need help with? _____

4. Return to the Knowledge Rating Chart at the beginning of this lesson. Complete column 3. How have your responses changed?

appropriate   although   circumstance   **appear**

basis   **challenge**   rely   content   critical

appear   consequence   **emphasize**   express

outcome   consistent   determine   represent

critical   symbol   **sufficient**   recognize   rely

Vocabulary Knowledge Rating Chart

How well do you know the words? Use the numbers to rate your knowledge of the vocabulary words. Follow the teacher's directions.

4 = I know the word. I know it well enough to teach it to someone else.
3 = The word is familiar. I think I know what it means.
2 = I have heard the word, but I'm not sure what it means.
1 = I don't know the word at all.

	My rating before instruction	I think the word means	My rating after instruction
appear			
challenge			
emphasize			
outcome			
sufficient			

Word Meaning Chart

Complete the chart. Follow the teacher's directions.

appear *(verb)* /uh PEER/
To **appear** means that something or someone can be seen.

EXAMPLES

When the full moon _____ in the sky, it seemed so close you could touch it.

Class Example: _____

My Example: When the fire engine **appeared** in front of our building, _____

challenge *(verb)* /CHAL inj/
To **challenge** is to ask someone to test his or her ability to do something difficult.

EXAMPLES

In the wild, a male lion often _____ other males who enter his territory.

Class Example: _____

My Example: A specific thing that **challenges** me is _____

emphasize *(verb)* /EM fuh sahyz/
To **emphasize** is to show that something is very important.

EXAMPLES

We underline words to _____ them.

Class Example: _____

My Example: Teachers often **emphasize** _____

outcome *(noun)* /OUT kuhm/
An **outcome** is the result of an action or event.

EXAMPLES

The _____ of the election was unexpected and surprised many people.

Class Example: _____

My Example: One **outcome** I expect from studying vocabulary is _____

sufficient *(adjective)* /suh FISH uhnt/
Sufficient means enough or adequate.

EXAMPLES

Do you have _____ emergency supplies to last several days?

Class Example: _____

My Example: When I get a **sufficient** amount of sleep, _____

Exercise 1 Use the Words

Complete each sentence. Write the correct form of the vocabulary word in the blank space.

1. Mr. Ziegler _____ his students to read at least one more book than was required for the class.

2. Doctors consistently _____ the benefit of exercise, a healthy diet, and regular physical checkups.

3. The bank executive was asked to _____ at the meeting to answer questions about the availability of loans.

4. Why did the judge determine the evidence was not _____ to take the case to trial?

5. The _____ of last night's soccer match was a cause for celebration among the many fans.

Exercise 2 Complete the Sentences

These sentences have been started for you. They are not complete. Complete them with your own words.

1. If a UFO appeared in my yard, I would _____

_____

2. When talking to young people about safe driving, it is important

to emphasize _____

_____

3. Being part of a team challenges me to _____

_____

_____

4. One thing we can do to stay healthy is to get a sufficient amount of

_____

_____

5. Friends who have an argument can reach a positive outcome if

_____

_____

Words at Work

Circle the best answer to each multiple choice question below. Then write a brief response to the question that follows. Write your answers in complete sentences.

1. Kenneth had a meeting with his manager to review his job performance. He was happy with the outcome of the meeting. Why did the outcome please him?

   (A) His manager told him a funny story.

   (B) His manager offered him coffee and donuts.

   (C) His manager gave him a good review and a raise.

   Describe an experience when you were pleased with the outcome of a meeting or

   conversation. _____

   _____

   _____

2. Arnold works 40 hours a week and gets paid on a weekly basis. Last week, a mistake appeared on his pay check. He was paid for 42 hours. What should he do?

   (A) cash the check and keep the money

   (B) report the mistake to the payroll department

   (C) tell his coworker about the mistake

   What would you do if a mistake appeared on your paycheck or grade slip? Has this ever

   happened to you? Explain. _____

   _____

   _____

3. Janette applied for a job in a retail store. She is preparing for her interview. What should she emphasize during the interview?

   (A) the classes she's taking in school

   (B) her experience as a cashier

   (C) her interests and other activities

   What would you emphasize during a job interview? _____

   _____

   _____

4. Tanya recently started a new job in customer service. Although it is an interesting job, it sometimes challenges her patience. Why does this job challenge Tanya?

   (A) Her coworkers are helpful.

   (B) Customers can often be angry and rude.

   (C) She is learning new job skills.

   When starting something new, what challenges you? _____

   _____

Exercise 4 · Word Families

Most words are part of a family of words. Study the word families on this page. Then fill in the missing words in the sentences below using the words from this lesson. Use the correct form of each word to complete the sentences.

---

appear *(verb)*

- **appearance** *(noun)*
  Dan's appearance at the party was unexpected.

challenge *(verb)*

- **challenge** *(noun)*
  One challenge facing the country is how to reduce energy usage.

- **challenging** *(adjective)*
  Chess is a challenging game that requires great mental skill.

emphasize *(verb)*

- **emphasis** *(noun)*
  The clerk repeated the date and time for emphasis.

sufficient *(adjective)*

- **sufficiently** *(adverb)*
  Doctors believe that vaccines sufficiently protect infants against measles.

- **self-sufficient** *(adjective)*
  Countries that are self-sufficient can meet the needs of their citizens.

---

1. The _____ of the training session for the hotel staff was on fire safety.

2. Working, going to school, and raising children are _____ responsibilities.

3. My brother's band has been asked to make an _____ at the music festival.

4. Masako operates her own business and considers herself to be an independent and

   _____ person.

5. Solomon easily passed the exam to become a barber because he studied consistently and

   was _____ prepared.

Milo of Kroton

Milo of Kroton was a famous wrestler in ancient Greece 2,500 years ago. He was very strong

and his physical _____ was quite impressive. He liked to play games that
                                    6.

_____ his strength. In one game, he spread out the fingers on his right
            7.

hand. Then he _____ people to bend his fingers. However, no one was
                          8.

_____ strong enough to bend even his little finger.
            9.

Nature and the environment are part of a country's wealth.

Exercise 5   What Do You Think?

Read each question and write a brief answer. Explain your answers in complete sentences.

1. Do Americans put sufficient emphasis on protecting nature and the environment?

   _____

   _____

   _____

2. When will an outcome be more successful—when someone challenges you to do something or when you challenge yourself?

   _____

   _____

   _____

3. Would you appear on television to express your opinions about the outcome of an election?

   _____

   _____

   _____

Reading Connection

Read the following passage and answer the questions.

The Purple Cow: A Poem by Gelett Burgess

A poem is a very special way for writers to express themselves. These writers, or poets, find ways to use as few words as possible to express their ideas. They experiment with the sounds of words and the rhythms the words make when they are put together.

Poets try to find words that make readers see a picture in their mind, or feel an emotion in their heart. Sometimes, a poem is serious or sad. Sometimes, it is funny. A poem always challenges the reader to think about an idea in a different way.

In 1896, Gelett Burgess wrote a four-line poem about a purple cow. A purple cow seems like a silly idea for a poem, but the poem is still well-known more than 100 years after it was written. Why did Mr. Burgess write the poem? Was he challenging us to think about something in a different way?

I never saw a Purple Cow,

I never hope to see one;

But I can tell you, anyhow,

I'd rather see than be one!

1. Has a purple cow ever appeared to the poet?

_____

_____

_____

2. What does the poet emphasize at the end of the poem?

_____

_____

_____

3. What is the poet feeling in this poem? Does he give us sufficient information in the poem for us to determine his feeling?

_____

_____

_____

appropriate although circumstance **appear** basis **challenge** rely on content critical appear consequence **emphasize** express **outcome** consistent determine represent critical symbol **sufficient** recognize rely on

New Word List

☐ appear

☐ challenge

☐ emphasize

☐ outcome

☐ sufficient

Review Word List

☐ _____

☐ _____

☐ _____

☐ _____

☐ _____

Exercise 7 # Writing Connection

Write a brief response to each question. Use words from this lesson or previous lessons in your answer. Write your answers in complete sentences.

Describe a situation in which the outcome was not what you expected. What was the situation? What was the outcome?

_____

_____

_____

_____

_____

Think of a person you know who is self-sufficient. Explain what makes that person self-sufficient.

_____

_____

_____

_____

_____

Exercise 8 # Reflection

Think about the words you have studied in this lesson.

1. Which words did you enjoy learning? _____

2. Select one word and imagine where you will use the word. Explain the situation.

_____

_____

3. Which words do you still need help with? _____

4. Return to the Knowledge Rating Chart at the beginning of this lesson. Complete column 3. How have your responses changed?

Activity 1 ## Ask Questions

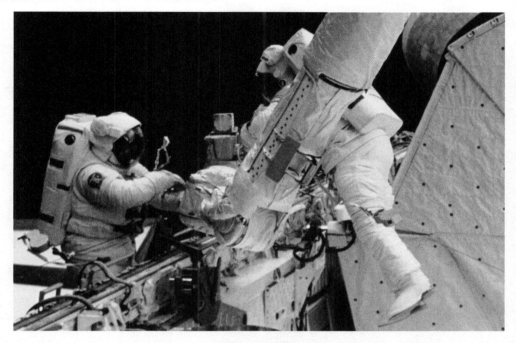

Look at the picture. Imagine you have the opportunity to ask the astronauts about their journey in space. Write at least five questions you want to ask them. Use one or more of the vocabulary words you have studied in this unit in each question. <u>Underline</u> each vocabulary word you use. Some of your questions can begin with *Who, What, When, Where, Why* or *How.*

Example: How did you feel when Earth appeared outside your window?

_____

_____

_____

_____

_____

_____

_____

_____

_____

_____

_____

_____

WORD BANK

ALTHOUGH
APPEAR
APPROPRIATE
BASIS
CHALLENGE
CIRCUMSTANCE
CONSEQUENCE
CONSISTENT
CONTENT
CRITICAL
DETERMINE
EMPHASIZE
EXPRESS
OUTCOME
PHASE
RECOGNIZE
RELY
REPRESENT
SUFFICIENT
SYMBOL

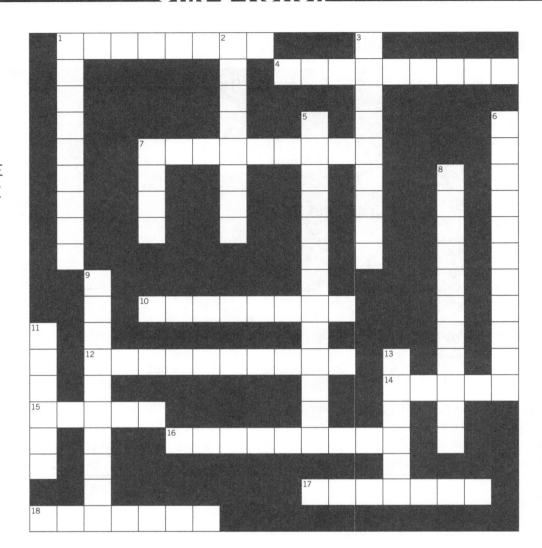

Activity 2 Puzzle

ACROSS

1. The economy is a _____ issue today.
4. Did the mechanic _____ the problem?
7. We did not _____ our old neighborhood.
10. Please list the _____ on top of the box.
12. Is there _____ time to watch the entire movie?
14. The last _____ of this project was the hardest.
15. On what _____ did you make your decision?
16. Driving teachers _____ the need to wear seat belts.
17. Did everyone get to _____ an opinion?
18. What was the _____ of the contract talks?

DOWN

1. Did Rudy _____ you to run the 10K race?
2. _____ it rained, we went on our hike.
3. Two senators _____ each state in the U.S. Senate.
5. The judge wants to know the _____ of the case before meeting the lawyers.
6. What is the _____ of losing a library book?
7. I _____ on my alarm clock to wake up.
8. It is not _____ to chew gum in class.
9. A garden should have _____ sunshine.
11. An olive branch is a _____ of peace.
13. When the sky gets dark, the stars _____.

Activity 3   Synonyms

Complete these sentences. Use the correct form of the vocabulary word that means the same as the word in parentheses.

Example: Paul _____expressed_____ (*showed*) his concern after the accident.

1. People _____ (*identify*) the Statue of Liberty as a symbol of freedom.

2. Did the judge _____ (*decide*) if the consequences were appropriate?

3. The coach _____ (*depends*) on the team captain to be a leader.

Activity 4   Antonyms

Complete these sentences. Use the correct form of the vocabulary word that means the opposite of the word or words in parentheses.

Example: _____Consistent_____ (*not regular*) exercise on a daily basis challenged Rita.

1. The outcome of the game was _____ (*unimportant*).

2. Is sending a plant an _____ (*not correct*) expression of sympathy?

3. It is important to get _____ (*not enough*) sleep before a test.

Activity 5   Use the Vocabulary Words

Complete the paragraph using the correct forms of the vocabulary words from this unit.

The Boston Tea Party

In the 1760s, England passed new laws to tax the American colonies. The colonists

_____ that the new taxes were unfair. However, England did not
    1.

_____ the rights of the Americans. This was the _____
    2.   **3.**

for the colonists' anger. The Tea Act was one of the most _____
                                                                    4.

laws. The colonists _____ their disapproval by throwing 342 boxes
                               5.

of British tea into Boston Harbor. This event became known as the Boston Tea Party.

_____ there was no positive _____, the Boston Tea
     6.   **7.**

Party became a _____ of American opposition to British rule.
                      8.

Unit 2

point
resource
approximately
strategy
directly
considerable
concept
objective
complex
effect
omit
develop
persistent
analyze
apply
initial
relate
modify
unless
achieve

achieve apply complex approximately omit point develop concept **analyze** considerable **effect** initial directly modify unless strategy point omit relate **objective** unless relate **persistent** resource apply

Vocabulary Knowledge Rating Chart

How well do you know the words? Use the numbers to rate your knowledge of the vocabulary words. Follow the teacher's directions.

4 = I know the word. I know it well enough to teach it to someone else.
3 = The word is familiar. I think I know what it means.
2 = I have heard the word, but I'm not sure what it means.
1 = I don't know the word at all.

	My rating before instruction	I think the word means	My rating after instruction
achieve			
analyze			
effect			
objective			
persistent			

Word Meaning Chart

Complete the chart. Follow the teacher's directions.

achieve *(verb)* /uh CHEEV/
To **achieve** means to succeed by using effort or skill.

EXAMPLES

Martin Luther King Jr.'s goal was to _____ equality for all people.

Class Example: _____

My Example: One goal I hope to **achieve** this year is _____

analyze *(verb)* /AN I ahyz/
To **analyze** means to examine something carefully to understand it.

EXAMPLES

The city council _____ the accident reports to determine if a stop sign was needed.

Class Example: _____

My Example: To help their students, teachers often **analyze** _____

effect *(noun)* /ih FEKT/
An **effect** is the change that results from an action by someone or something.

EXAMPLES

Mr. Hussein noticed that helping his son with his homework had a positive _____ on their relationship.

Class Example: _____

My Example: One **effect** a rainy day has on me is _____

objective *(noun)* /uhb JEK tiv/
An **objective** is a goal or purpose.

EXAMPLES

One _____ of learning vocabulary is to be able to express yourself more clearly when speaking and writing.

Class Example: _____

My Example: My **objective** for saving money is _____

persistent *(adjective)* /per SIS tuhnt/
Persistent means not giving up or lasting a longer time than usual.

EXAMPLES

A _____ person does not accept "no" for an answer.

Class Example: _____

My Example: A **persistent** problem in our community is _____

Exercise 1 Use the Words

Complete each sentence. Write the correct form of the vocabulary word in the blank space.

1. The scientists _____ the available research to determine the age of the dinosaur bones.

2. What were the _____ of increasing the number of students in every class?

3. One of the general's _____ was to protect the town.

4. Michael Jordan _____ great success during his basketball career.

5. The _____ pain in his tooth was the reason Rahsaan went to the dentist.

Exercise 2 Complete the Sentences

These sentences have been started for you. They are not complete. Complete them with your own words.

1. For me, one effect of higher gas prices is _____

   _____

   _____

2. I have to be persistent when I _____

   _____

   _____

3. A teacher can help me achieve success by _____

   _____

   _____

4. One objective of getting x-rays and other medical tests is _____

   _____

   _____

5. I analyze my behavior because _____

   _____

   _____

Words at Work

Circle the best answer to each multiple choice question below. Then write a brief response to the question that follows. Write your answers in complete sentences.

___

1. The new restaurant owners made a few changes. One change now requires all employees to be in uniform before punching in on the time clock. What is an effect of this change?

   (A) Employees need to get to work earlier to change.

   (B) Employees may need to buy second uniform.

   (C) Employees have to wash their uniforms more often.

   What was a change at school or work that had an effect on you? How did you respond?

   _____

   _____

2. Stephen's desk is near the copy machine. The persistent noise of the machine and the conversations of the people using it bother him. He can't concentrate. Stephen can't change desks. What can he do?

   (A) ask people not to talk

   (B) ask his manager if he can wear earphones

   (C) ask the manager to buy a quieter copy machine

   Does persistent noise from a television, radio, or other people bother you? How do you

   respond? _____

   _____

3. The company has received several complaints about their telephone answering system. How will the company analyze the problem?

   (A) test each part of the system

   (B) put a new message on the answering system

   (C) replace all the phones

   Why is it necessary to analyze a problem? _____

   _____

4. "Our key objective," the manager told the employees, "is to make sure that the customer wants to come back. The best way to do that is to see that a customer never leaves with a question." What could Ms. Jackson do if she does not know the answer to a customer's question?

   (A) tell the customer to ask a different question

   (B) give the customer an answer he or she wants to hear

   (C) tell the customer she will ask someone who knows the answer

   How does answering questions achieve the manager's objective? _____

   _____

Word Families

Most words are part of a family of words. Study the word families on this page. Then fill in the missing words in the sentences below using the words from this lesson. Use the correct form of each word to complete the sentences.

---

achieve *(verb)*

- achievement *(noun)*
  Winning a medal in the Olympics is a major achievement.

analyze *(verb)*

- analysis *(noun)*
  The analysis of the rocks and other information from the moon took years.

effect *(noun)*

- effective *(adjective)*
  Aspirin is effective in reducing fever.
- effectively *(adverb)*
  Ms. Perez effectively taught her students how to write an essay.

persistent *(adjective)*

- persist *(verb)*
  If you persist, you will find a job although it may be difficult.
- persistently *(adverb)*
  Rosa Parks persistently refused to give up her seat on the bus.
- persistence *(noun)*
  A runner needs persistence to complete a marathon.

---

1. What's an _____ method to learn how to play the guitar?

2. Because of the detective's _____, the criminal was found and arrested.

3. Mr. Bitar was proud of his wife's _____. She earned a college degree.

4. Firefighters must _____ fight heat and smoke to put out fires.

5. When will the budget _____ be ready for the vice president?

6. Lucinda _____ and finally got the charges reversed on her phone bill.

7. My new dishwasher cleans dishes more _____ than my old one.

Women's Right to Vote

Women received the right to vote in 1920. It took the _____ of many
8.

women for many years to _____ that objective. One woman,
9.

Susan B. Anthony, was an _____ leader. She communicated
10.

_____ and was able to organize other women. She _____
11.   **12.**

the conditions and situations of women. She determined that nothing would improve until women

could vote. She is remembered for this important _____.
13.

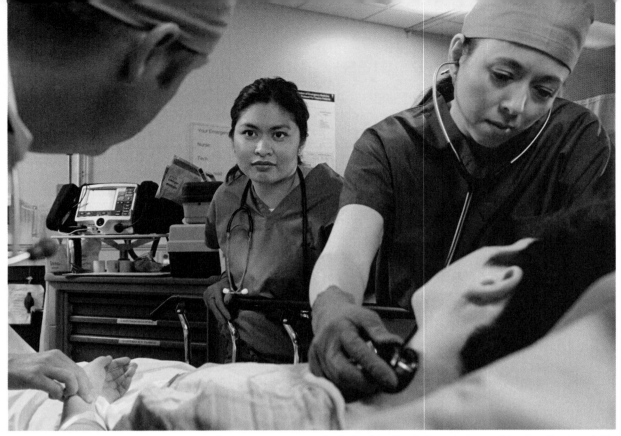

An emergency room doctor's objective is to examine and treat patients quickly.

Exercise 5 What Do You Think?

Read each question and write a brief answer. Explain your answers in complete sentences.

1. Is it necessary for a doctor to analyze information before treating a patient?

_____

_____

_____

2. Would students achieve success if schools changed to a four-day week schedule? What would be the effects of that change?

_____

_____

_____

3. Is it better to keep objectives the same or to change them to achieve success?

_____

_____

_____

Reading Connection

Read the following passage and answer the questions.

Take a Picture

Photography is part of our everyday lives. We see photographs everywhere. They are in newspapers, books, and magazines. They even appear on restaurant menus. Many people keep photos of their family and friends on their cell phones and computers.

However, photography did not exist 200 years ago. People relied on artists to draw or paint a picture of a person or a place. In the 1800s, however, people began to experiment with ways to create images using light, not paint.

The first photograph was made in France in 1826. The photograph shows a view from a window of a farmhouse on a summer afternoon. It took eight hours to make the photograph. The photograph was made on a piece of metal.

One of the first photographs of a human being was taken in Philadelphia in 1839. Robert Cornelius was interested in photography. He set up a camera and took this picture of himself.

The process for taking early photographs was difficult. Photographers could only take one picture at a time because cameras were not automatic. It also took several minutes for the camera to take one picture. Because of that, people had to remain perfectly still. If they moved, the photograph would be ruined.

Today, anyone with a camera or even a cell phone can take a photograph quickly and easily. It is not necessary to be familiar with photography to take a good picture. Today's digital cameras adjust the focus and color of the picture.

1. Where did Mr. Cornelius take his photograph?

_____

_____

2. What effect did movement have on early photographs like the one of Mr. Cornelius?

_____

_____

3. Do you think early photographers had to be persistent to achieve a good photograph?

_____

_____

achieve apply complex approximately omit
point develop concept **analyze** considerable
effect initial directly modify unless
strategy point omit relate **objective**
unless relate **persistent** resource apply

New Word List

☐ achieve

☐ analyze

☐ effect

☐ objective

☐ persistent

Review Word List

☐ _____

☐ _____

☐ _____

☐ _____

☐ _____

Exercise 7 Writing Connection

Write a brief response to each question. Use words from this lesson or previous lessons in your answer. Write your answers in complete sentences.

Give an example of a time you analyzed information to make a decision. How did your analysis help you make the decision? Was it effective?

_____

_____

_____

_____

_____

How do you respond to a person who is persistent with you? For example, what effect does a persistent salesperson or teacher have on you?

_____

_____

_____

_____

_____

Exercise 8 Reflection

Think about the words you have studied in this lesson.

1. Which words did you enjoy learning? _____

2. Select one word and imagine where you will use the word. Explain the situation.

_____

_____

3. Which words do you still need help with? _____

4. Return to the Knowledge Rating Chart at the beginning of this lesson. Complete column 3. How have your responses changed?

omit achieve **apply** complex approximately

develop analyze concept considerable

modify unless effect **initial** directly

objective **strategy** point omit relate

persistent relate resource apply **unless**

Vocabulary Knowledge Rating Chart

How well do you know the words? Use the numbers to rate your knowledge of the vocabulary words. Follow the teacher's directions.

4 = I know the word. I know it well enough to teach it to someone else.
3 = The word is familiar. I think I know what it means.
2 = I have heard the word, but I'm not sure what it means.
1 = I don't know the word at all.

	My rating before instruction	I think the word means	My rating after instruction
apply			
develop			
initial			
strategy			
unless			

Word Meaning Chart

Complete the chart. Follow the teacher's directions.

apply *(verb)* /uh PLAHY/ To **apply** means to use knowledge or ability in a specific situation.

EXAMPLES

After you study the spelling rules, you need to _____ them when you write.

Class Example: _____

My Example: I **apply** my computer skills when _____

develop *(verb)* /dih VEL uhp/ To **develop** is to create or to grow into something larger or better.

EXAMPLES

Lifting weights _____ strong bones and muscles.

Class Example: _____

My Example: I can **develop** my writing skills by _____

initial *(adjective)* /ih NISH uhl/ **Initial** means at the beginning or first.

EXAMPLES

The _____ report said the fire burned five acres. We learned later the total was 20 acres.

Class Example: _____

My Example: When I heard that my teacher won the lottery, my **initial** reaction was _____

strategy *(noun)* /STRAT i jee/ A **strategy** is a plan of action or way to reach a goal.

EXAMPLES

The coach's new defensive _____ worked. The team won the game.

Class Example: _____

My Example: You will need a **strategy** if you want to _____

unless *(conjunction)* /uhn LES/ **Unless** means except when or if not.

EXAMPLES

The doctor plans to operate _____ the patient has a temperature.

Class Example: _____

My Example: **Unless** it rains, _____

Use the Words

Complete each sentence. Write the correct form of the vocabulary word in the blank space.

1. The director of the preschool will _____ a plan to expand childcare options for working parents.

2. The president will sign a new law that Congress passes _____ he strongly disagrees with it.

3. George's Barber Shop is working on an advertising _____ to get younger customers interested in its services.

4. Do the new monthly rates _____ to all members or only to new members?

5. Our _____ efforts to connect the older printers to the new computer were not successful.

Exercise 2 Complete the Sentences

These sentences have been started for you. They are not complete. Complete them with your own words.

1. A study strategy that works for me is _____

_____

2. One thing I can do to develop my financial skills is _____

_____

_____

3. A rule that usually applies only to children is _____

_____

_____

4. Although my initial response to my new neighbor was negative,

_____

_____

5. Unless I have a high school diploma or a GED certificate, _____

_____

_____

Words at Work

Circle the best answer to each multiple choice question below. Then write a brief response to the question that follows. Write your answers in complete sentences.

1. There is a sign near the time clock that reads, "All employees should park in Lot 2 unless there is a sales meeting. During sales meetings, employees should use Lot 4." How would you explain this sign to a new employee?

   (A) Employees can't park in Lot 4 if there is a meeting.

   (B) Employees can park in Lot 2 if there is a meeting.

   (C) Employees can park in Lot 4 if there is a meeting

   Think of a situation when you can't do something unless something else happens.

   _____

   _____

2. Julia's initial impression after her first day at work was not positive. She did not find her coworkers very friendly. However, after a couple of weeks, Julia described her coworkers as nice and helpful. What changed her initial impression?

   (A) Everyone had too much work.

   (B) She was invited to join a group for lunch.

   (C) She did not know the names of her coworkers.

   Are initial impressions usually accurate? Why or why not? _____

   _____

   _____

3. Mrs. King joined a parent committee at her children's elementary school. The committee is developing a program to offer after-school activities for the students. How can Mrs. King help the committee develop this program?

   (A) She can offer appropriate ideas for activities.

   (B) She can pick up her children after school.

   (C) She can analyze the amount of homework assignments.

   When have you helped develop a project, plan, or something else at work or school? _____

   _____

   _____

4. The manager at CD Designs developed a new strategy to reduce absences. The initial response from employees was positive. What did the strategy include?

   (A) a warning after three absences

   (B) a doctor's note after two absences

   (C) two hours of vacation after a month of no absences

   What is another strategy to reduce absences or tardiness? _____

   _____

Word Families

Most words are part of a family of words. Study the word families on this page. Then fill in the missing words in the sentences below using the words from this lesson. Use the correct form of each word to complete the sentences.

---

apply *(verb)*

- application *(noun)*
  The application of the new technology improved satellite communication.

initial *(adjective)*

- initially *(adverb)*
  Mr. Clark initially had no pain, so the diagnosis took longer than usual.

- initiate *(verb)*
  My sister initiated the divorce, not her husband.

develop *(verb)*

- development *(noun)*
  The development of the automobile was a major achievement of the 20th century.

- developed *(adjective)*
  Kareem has great talent, but his skills are not developed.

- developing *(adjective)*
  Many people were not aware of the developing financial crisis.

strategy *(noun)*

- strategic *(adjective)*
  It was a strategic decision for the small restaurant to add a children's menu.

---

1. The _____ of farming machines reduced the need for human labor.

2. The salesperson _____ told us that today was the last day of the sale. However, she told us later that it lasts until Sunday.

3. Do you think downtown is a _____ location for the new store?

4. Children need constant reminders because their manners are not completely

   _____ .

5. Ace Home Designs _____ an employee-of-the-month program.

6. Did you know that duct tape is a practical _____ of space technology?

Heart Health

There are several _____ you can use to prevent heart disease. Be
                          7.

physically active. _____ a plan for regular exercise. Learn which foods
                          8.

are best for you. _____ this knowledge to your family's food choices.
                          9.

Don't smoke. Tobacco can lead to the _____ of heart problems. Make
                                          10.

_____ decisions now to prevent painful consequences later.
        11.

Nature and its wonders are available for all of us to enjoy.

Exercise 5 # What Do You Think?

Read each question and write a brief answer. Explain your answers in complete sentences.

1. Is it necessary to develop a national strategy to protect wildlife?

_____

_____

_____

2. Should individual circumstances determine how a law is applied?

_____

_____

_____

3. As people get older, is it necessary for them to develop new skills? Or should they find new strategies for applying the skills they already have? Give examples.

_____

_____

_____

Reading Connection

Read the following passage and answer the questions.

A Day in the Civil Rights Movement

February 1, 1960, is an important day in the history of the American Civil Rights Movement.

Four black college students sat down at a lunch counter at the Woolworth's store in Greensboro, North Carolina. In 1960, black people were not allowed to sit at lunch counters in stores like Woolworth's. Only white people could sit at counters and eat. Blacks had to stand and eat their lunch.

Black students at the Woolworth's lunch counter.

The four black students were Ezell A. Blair Jr., David L. Richmond, Joseph A. McNeil, and Franklin E. McCain. They asked for service. Their request was denied. The young men were asked to leave. They politely refused. They continued sitting at the counter. This was how they protested segregation at lunch counters.

The protest was called a "sit-in." A sit-in is a nonviolent way for people to show that they strongly disagree with something and that they want it to change.

The next day, the four students returned and 27 more people joined the sit-in. Four days later, there were 300 people. The sit-in at Woolworth's led to other sit-ins in other parts of North Carolina and other states. Sit-ins became a powerful symbol of the movement to end racial discrimination in the United States.

Six months later, the Woolworth's lunch counter was desegregated. Black and white people could finally sit at the same counter and eat lunch in Greensboro.

1. The students refused to leave the lunch counter unless something changed at Woolworth's. What did they want changed?

   _____

   _____

   _____

2. What was the outcome that developed from the initial sit-in in Greensboro in February of 1960?

   _____

   _____

   _____

3. What is the strategy of a sit-in?

   _____

   _____

apply
develop analyze concept considerable
modify unless effect initial directly
objective strategy point omit relate
persistent relate resource apply unless

New Word List

- ☐ apply
- ☐ develop
- ☐ initial
- ☐ strategy
- ☐ unless

Review Word List

- ☐ _____
- ☐ _____
- ☐ _____
- ☐ _____
- ☐ _____

Exercise 7 Writing Connection

Write a brief response to each question. Use words from this lesson or previous lessons in your answer. Write your answers in complete sentences.

Reflect on a time when you had to revise an initial thought, impression, or reaction. What was it? What changed your initial response?

_____
_____
_____
_____

Unless children are given responsibilities, they will not develop into independent adults. Give one example to explain this.

_____
_____
_____
_____

Exercise 8 Reflection

Think about the words you have studied in this lesson.

1. Which words did you enjoy learning? _____

2. Select one word and imagine where you will use the word. Explain the situation.

_____
_____

3. Which words do you still need help with? _____

4. Return to the Knowledge Rating Chart at the beginning of this lesson. Complete column 3. How have your responses changed?

achieve apply **complex** approximately omit

analyze develop considerable **concept**

effect initial **directly** modify unless

point objective strategy omit relate

persistent unless resource **relate** apply

Vocabulary Knowledge Rating Chart

How well do you know the words? Use the numbers to rate your knowledge of the vocabulary words. Follow the teacher's directions.

4 = I know the word. I know it well enough to teach it to someone else.
3 = The word is familiar. I think I know what it means.
2 = I have heard the word, but I'm not sure what it means.
1 = I don't know the word at all.

	My rating before instruction	I think the word means	My rating after instruction
complex			
concept			
directly			
point			
relate			

Word Meaning Chart

Complete the chart. Follow the teacher's directions.

complex *(adjective)* /KOM pleks/ — **Complex** means having many parts or being difficult to understand.

EXAMPLES

The insurance policy is long and difficult to understand. It is a _____ document.

Class Example: _____

My Example: A **complex** issue in the world today is _____

concept *(noun)* /KON sept/ — A **concept** is the idea of what or how something is.

EXAMPLES

It is essential to understand the _____ of homelessness before offering a solution.

Class Example: _____

My Example: Children often have no **concept** of _____

directly *(adverb)* /dih REKT lee/ — **Directly** means with nothing or no one in between.

EXAMPLES

Economic conditions can _____ influence a person's attitude toward life.

Class Example: _____

My Example: A job that works **directly** with customers is _____

point *(noun)* /point/ — A **point** is one idea, the most important idea, or the purpose of something.

EXAMPLES

The _____ of the video was to convince people to wear seat belts at all times.

Class Example: _____

My Example: One **point** I want to make about our city is _____

relate *(verb)* /ri LEYT/ — To **relate** means to make a connection to someone or something.

EXAMPLES

How does having a diploma _____ to getting a good job?

Class Example: _____

My Example: Young people often **relate** to famous athletes because _____

Use the Words

Complete each sentence. Write the correct form of the vocabulary word in the blank space.

1. Research shows that smoking _____ causes lung cancer.

2. The politician said, "I believe in the _____ of not fixing what is not broken."

3. I agreed with all the _____ the writer made in her article about global warming except for the last one.

4. Oil spills in the ocean are _____ problems that have consequences for many years.

5. How does eating a healthy breakfast _____ to a student's performance in school?

Complete the Sentences

These sentences have been started for you. They are not complete. Complete them with your own words.

1. A famous person I relate to is _____ because _____
   _____

2. If it is going to rain, what is the point of _____
   _____
   _____

3. It is important for children to speak directly to their parents when _____
   _____
   _____

4. One science or math concept I know is _____
   _____
   _____

5. When I come to a complex question on a test, I _____
   _____
   _____
   _____

Words at Work

Circle the best answer to each multiple choice question below. Then write a brief response to the question that follows. Write your answers in complete sentences.

1. The Sunshine Café ran out of eggs and other breakfast items yesterday morning. Mr. Baxter was directly responsible for the situation. What tells you that this is true?

   (A) His secretary was sick.   **(B)** His job is to order supplies.   **(C)** The cooks used too many eggs.

   What is a waitress directly responsible for? What is a cook directly responsible for? _____

   _____

   _____

2. The employees at a sporting goods store were told that the store phone and computer could only be used for calls and emails that related to store business. Kerry is a new employee. What does this mean for her?

   (A) Kerry should not answer the phone.   **(B)** Kerry can e-mail her friends during breaks.   **(C)** Kerry can call customers about their orders.

   What is another example of an activity that is related to business? _____

   _____

   _____

3. Ms. Chan just finished the monthly schedule for her company. It usually takes several hours because it is quite complex. Why?

   (A) The schedule is for all shifts and employees.   **(B)** The schedule is usually printed on colored paper.   **(C)** A copy of the schedule is given to each employee.

   Think of another schedule that is complex. Why is it complex? _____

   _____

   _____

4. Jamal asked his manager at the photography shop about a refund given to a customer. "What is the point of giving the customer a refund if it was not the store's fault?" Jamal asked. What point did Jamal's manager make when he responded?

   (A) The point is customer satisfaction.   **(B)** The point is not to listen to customer complaints.   **(C)** The point is to be popular with customers.

   What points do customers make when they want a refund? _____

   _____

   _____

Word Families

Most words are part of a family of words. Study the word families on this page. Then fill in the missing words in the sentences below using the words from this lesson. Use the correct form of each word to complete the sentences.

---

complex *(adjective)*

- **complexity** *(noun)*
  Because of the complexity of legal documents, most people need help to understand them.

concept *(noun)*

- **conceptualize** *(verb)*
  Thomas Jefferson was able to conceptualize liberty and express it in the Declaration of Independence.

directly *(adverb)*

- **direct** *(adjective)*
  Children need to have direct interaction with other children their own age.

- **direct** *(verb)*
  "I want to direct your attention to the remodeled bathroom," said the real estate agent.

relate *(verb)*

- **related** *(adjective)*
  Air pollution and global warming are related issues.

- **relation** *(noun)*
  Is it true that women's pay is often lower in relation to men's?

- **relationship** *(noun)*
  There is a relationship between the physical condition of soccer players and their ability to play well.

---

1. Lew's job put him in _____ contact with customers every day.

2. People _____ happiness in different ways.

3. How are good physical health and a positive attitude _____?

4. The _____ of the peace talks required many hours of discussion.

5. Where do I _____ my questions about the citizenship process?

6. Is it true that women's pay is often lower in _____ to men's?

Prohibition

At the end of the 19th century, many people believed that crime was _____
                                                                              7.
to drinking alcohol. They thought the solution to this _____ problem was
                                                                   8.
to make alcohol illegal. This _____ became known as Prohibition.
                                        9.
However, people were not able to _____ the consequences of Prohibition.
                                              10.
It _____ increased crime. The law was changed 13 years later.
       11.

College graduation is a major achievement.

Exercise 5   What Do You Think?

Read each question and write a brief answer. Explain your answers in complete sentences.

1. What is the point of going to college? Is it getting job, or is there another objective?

   _____

   _____

2. The concept of the American Dream is that anyone can achieve success in the United States. Is this concept directly related to the large number of people who want to come to the United States?

   _____

   _____

   _____

3. Is finding a job more directly related to whom you know or to your job skills and experience?

   _____

   _____

Reading Connection

Read the following passage and answer the questions.

Roman Numerals

Why are numbers important? People have always needed a way to identify quantities for many purposes. Ancient people developed different symbols to represent quantities of the things in their lives. The ancient Romans developed their own system of numbers. We call them Roman numerals.

Roman numerals are written using different combinations of seven letters. However, there was no letter to represent zero. There were no fractions either. Roman numerals were used in Europe until about the 12th century. Then a new set of numbers was introduced to the Europeans by Arab traders. These numbers gradually replaced Roman numerals because they were easier to use. The new numbers were very similar to the numbers we use today. We call them Arabic numerals. The chart shows the seven Roman numerals and their Arabic equivalents.

Roman Numerals	
I = 1	C = 100
V = 5	D = 500
X = 10	M = 1000
L = 50	

Roman numerals are still used today in the United States for special purposes. An important historical event is often identified with a Roman numeral. One example is World War II (World War Two). The names of kings and queens include a Roman numeral, such as Queen Elizabeth II (Queen Elizabeth the Second). Pages in books are sometimes numbered using Roman numerals. Outlines are organized with Roman numerals. Another common use of Roman numerals is on clocks and wristwatches. Football fans will recognize Roman numerals when they watch the Super Bowl. The games are identified with Roman numerals. Which game is Super Bowl XXXVIII?

1. What is the concept of numbers? Why do people need numbers?

_____

_____

2. How are Roman numerals more complex than Arabic numerals?

_____

_____

3. How are Roman numerals directly related to American life today? Give two examples.

_____

_____

achieve apply **complex** approximately omit
analyze develop considerable **concept**
effect initial **directly** modify unless
point objective strategy omit relate
persistent unless resource **relate** apply

New Word List

☐ complex

☐ concept

☐ directly

☐ point

☐ relate

Review Word List

☐ _____

☐ _____

☐ _____

☐ _____

☐ _____

Writing Connection

Write a brief response to each question. Use words from this lesson or previous lessons in your answer. Write your answers in complete sentences.

Imagine you are called to give your opinion on a talk radio show. What is an issue that interests you or directly applies to you? Identify the issue and make two or three points about it that reflect your viewpoint.

_____

_____

_____

_____

_____

Describe your concept of outer space.

_____

_____

_____

_____

Reflection

Think about the words you have studied in this lesson.

1. Which words did you enjoy learning? _____

2. Select one word and imagine where you will use the word. Explain the situation.

_____

_____

3. Which words do you still need help with? _____

4. Return to the Knowledge Rating Chart at the beginning of this lesson. Complete column 3. How have your responses changed?

achieve apply complex **approximately**
considerable analyze develop concept
point effect initial **modify** directly unless
objective **omit** strategy develop point relate
persistent unless relate **resource** apply

Vocabulary Knowledge Rating Chart

How well do you know the words? Use the numbers to rate your knowledge of the vocabulary words. Follow the teacher's directions.

4 = I know the word. I know it well enough to teach it to someone else.
3 = The word is familiar. I think I know what it means.
2 = I have heard the word, but I'm not sure what it means.
1 = I don't know the word at all.

	My rating before instruction	I think the word means	My rating after instruction
approximately			
considerable			
modify			
omit			
resource			

Word Meaning Chart

Complete the chart. Follow the teacher's directions.

approximately *(adverb)* /uh PROK suh mit li/

Approximately means a little more or less than an exact number or amount.

EXAMPLES

The 705 bus will arrive in _____ 10 minutes.

Class Example: _____

My Example: The distance from my home to school is **approximately** _____

considerable *(adjective)* /kuhn SID er uh buhl/

Considerable means that something is large enough to be important or noticed.

EXAMPLES

Looking for a new job requires _____ effort.

Class Example: _____

My Example: It takes me a **considerable** amount of time to _____

modify *(verb)* /MOD uh fahy/

To **modify** means to make small changes to improve something.

EXAMPLES

The company _____ the toy to make it safe for infants.

Class Example: _____

My Example: The teacher **modified** our homework assignment by _____

omit *(verb)* /oh MIT/

To **omit** means not to include or to remove something or someone.

EXAMPLES

Ms. Rush apologized because she _____ Jasper's name from the graduation list.

Class Example: _____

My Example: My application was not complete because I **omitted** _____

resource *(noun)* /REE sohrs/

A **resource** is something available to be used and that benefits the user.

EXAMPLES

The library provides students with many different _____ to use.

Class Example: _____

My Example: Trees are a natural **resource**. Another natural resource is _____

Exercise 1 Use the Words

Complete each sentence. Write the correct form of the vocabulary word in the blank space.

1. Although the athlete was in _____ pain, she continued playing in the game.

2. The realtor asked the couple, "Do you have the financial _____ to buy a home now?"

3. The teacher asked the students to _____ question 15 on the biology test because it was written incorrectly.

4. Adam thinks he weighed _____ seven pounds when he was born.

5. Alicia _____ her diet to include more fruits and vegetables.

Exercise 2 Complete the Sentences

These sentences have been started for you. They are not complete. Complete them with your own words.

1. The last time I made chocolate chip cookies I omitted _____

   because _____

   _____

2. It costs approximately $10 to _____

   _____

   _____

3. My friends and I put together our resources to _____

   _____

   _____

4. Martin modified his exercise plan so he _____

   _____

   _____

5. After considerable thought, I decided _____

   _____

   _____

Words at Work

Circle the best answer to each multiple choice question below. Then write a brief response to the question that follows. Write your answers in complete sentences.

1. The Harbor Grill's menus were quite old, so the owner modified them. What did he do?

   (A) He copied the prices.   **(B)** He changed the prices.   **(C)** He analyzed the prices.

   What are two other ways to modify a menu? _____

   _____

   _____

2. The inventory list of toy parts needs to be updated. It is Matt's job to revise the list and omit any items that are no longer in the stockroom. What is Matt going to do to the list?

   (A) add items   **(B)** remove items   **(C)** order new items

   What is a reason to omit something from a list? Give an example. _____

   _____

   _____

3. Cheryl and Anita are working on a project at their children's school. It is very challenging because their resources are limited. What resources do they need?

   (A) paint and paper supplies   **(B)** parent-teacher meetings   **(C)** the school library

   Identify some resources you might need to have a classroom party. _____

   _____

   _____

4. Lester was looking in the classified ads for a job. He noticed that there were a considerable number of jobs that fit his skills and experience. How did that make Lester feel?

   (A) He was upset.   **(B)** He was disappointed.   **(C)** He was pleased.

   You learn that there are a considerable number of applicants for a job you want. What does that tell you? How will you respond? _____

   _____

   _____

Word Families

Most words are part of a family of words. Study the word families on this page. Then fill in the missing words in the sentences below using the words from this lesson. Use the correct form of each word to complete the sentences.

---

approximately *(adverb)*

- approximate *(adjective)*
  What is the approximate cost to feed a family of four?

considerable *(adjective)*

- considerably *(adverb)*
  Summer days are considerably longer with more hours of sunlight than winter days.

modify *(verb)*

- modification *(noun)*
  The vice-president approved the modifications made to the budget.

omit *(verb)*

- omission *(noun)*
  Lupe was upset with the omission of the date on the wedding invitation.

resource *(noun)*

- resourceful *(adjective)*
  If you need help, ask Jackie. She is very resourceful, especially using the Internet.

---

1. For spring break, the coach made _____ to the practice schedule.

2. The young boy is _____ tall for his age.

3. Because of the _____ of her Social Security number on the payroll form, Wanda did not get paid on time.

4. What is the _____ age of your house?

5. Students are encouraged to be _____ so they can learn to solve problems on their own.

Natural Resources

Everything we find in our environment is a natural _____. Water,
6.

plants, and minerals are examples. We can not _____ sunlight and air
7.

from the list. These are renewable resources. They can be easily replaced. Coal and oil, however,

are examples of non-renewable resources. They take a _____ long time to
8.

form in the earth. We need to make _____ to the way we use energy. If we
9.

are more _____ today, future generations may have the natural resources
10.

they need.

Heavy storms can cause considerable damage.

What Do You Think?

Read each question and write a brief answer. Explain your answers in complete sentences.

1. Is it possible for human beings to modify the weather if they have the appropriate resources?

   _____

   _____

   _____

2. With considerable time and patience, is it possible to modify another person's behavior?

   _____

   _____

   _____

3. Is it ever necessary to modify or omit information about yourself?

   _____

   _____

Reading Connection

Read the following passage and answer the questions.

The Regions of the United States

People who live in the United States have many things in common. However, Americans also think of themselves in relation to the region of the country they live in. A region is a large area that is defined by geography, history, and other things. Regions may have special foods or customs. People who live in certain regions may have different accents. There are five major regions of the United States. Use the map to locate each region as you read.

The Northeast The Northeast contains most of the original thirteen American colonies. It was the site of the American Revolution. Boston and Philadelphia are very important cities in U.S. history. New York City is the largest city in the country.

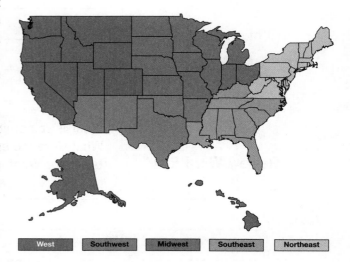

The Southeast The Southeast, or the South, has a significant history. Slavery was a major part of the South until the Civil War. Much of the war was fought in this region. Southern cooking is famous. Jazz came out of the South and helped to make New Orleans popular.

The Midwest Manufacturing and farming developed the Midwest. Detroit was the home of the American automobile industry. Kansas and North Dakota produce most of the nation's wheat. Chicago is the nation's third largest city.

The Southwest Large Native American and Latin American populations help define the Southwest. The Southwest contains much of the nation's desert land. It is the home of the Grand Canyon.

The West From the Rocky Mountains to the Pacific Ocean, this large region is quite diverse. In Wyoming and Montana, there are few people. However, Los Angeles is the country's second largest city. In Hawaii, Asian Americans are the largest ethnic group. The land varies from deserts to rainy forests in the Pacific Northwest.

All together, the regions of the United States create a richly diverse country.

1. What are some of the things that define a region? Can you think of something else that defines a region that the passage omitted?

_____

2. Which region of the country do you live in? What are some of its natural resources?

_____

3. It is approximately 2500 miles from New York City to Los Angeles. Imagine you are going to drive that considerable distance. Which regions would you like to see? Why?

_____

achieve apply complex **approximately**
considerable analyze develop concept
point effect initial **modify** directly unless
objective **omit** strategy develop point relate
persistent unless relate **resource** apply

New Word List

☐ approximately

☐ considerable

☐ modify

☐ omit

☐ resource

Review Word List

☐ _____

☐ _____

☐ _____

☐ _____

☐ _____

Exercise 7 # Writing Connection

Write a brief response to each question. Use words from this lesson or previous lessons in your answer. Write your answers in complete sentences.

Imagine you have been asked to help modify something at work or school. What is it—the registration process, break times, reporting absences, or something else? Describe your suggestions to modify it.

_____

_____

_____

_____

What is something you did that took considerable time and effort? What were the circumstances? Approximately, how long did it take you? What resources did you use?

_____

_____

_____

_____

Exercise 8 # Reflection

Think about the words you have studied in this lesson.

1. Which words did you enjoy learning? _____

2. Select one word and imagine where you will use the word. Explain the situation.

_____

_____

3. Which words do you still need help with? _____

4. Return to the Knowledge Rating Chart at the beginning of this lesson. Complete column 3. How are your responses changed?

Activity 1 ## Make Statements

Write five statements about the picture. Your statements can describe what you see or give an opinion. You can select a sentence starter from the chart to help you create interesting and different sentences. Use one or more of the vocabulary words you studied in this unit in each sentence. You may also use words from the previous unit. <u>Underline</u> each vocabulary word you use.

Example: It seems to me that it takes <u>considerable</u> practice to participate in a rodeo.

Make an observation:	Give an opinion:
There is/There are...	I think...
I notice that...	In my opinion...
It seems that...	It is important/It is essential...

_____

_____

_____

_____

_____

_____

_____

_____

WORD BANK

ACHIEVE
ANALYZE
APPLY
APPROXIMATELY
COMPLEX
CONCEPT
CONSIDERABLE
DEVELOP
DIRECTLY
EFFECT
INITIAL
MODIFY
OBJECTIVE
OMIT
PERSISTENT
POINT
RELATE
RESOURCE
STRATEGY
UNLESS

Activity 2 Puzzle

ACROSS

1. Why did the coach _____ his game plan?
8. The teacher explained the _____ math problem more than once.
9. It will take _____ two hours to drive to the lake.
14. You can not see the doctor _____ you have an appointment.
17. It is necessary to have a _____ to protect the environment.
18. Is Mark's fatigue a side _____ of his medication?
19. The test question asked the students to _____ the causes of the Civil War.
20. Martin Luther King Jr. believed in the _____ of nonviolence.

DOWN

2. I spoke _____ with the nurse.
3. Athletes want to _____ a gold medal.
4. I do not understand the _____ you made about health insurance.
5. How does diet _____ to behavior?
6. Coal is an important natural _____.
7. Be sure your forms are complete. Do not _____ anything.
10. Pam had a _____ cough for weeks.
11. Do not forget to _____ the rules of capitalization when you write.
12. _____ amounts of money are spent on political campaigns.
13. The company's _____ was to grow.
15. Did Tina _____ an interest in art?
16. Did the _____ phase of work begin?

Activity 3 Synonyms

Complete these sentences. Use the correct form of the vocabulary word that means the same as the word in parentheses.

Example: The committee spent _____*approximately*_____ (*about*) one week developing the safety plan.

1. Sometimes it is necessary to modify an _____ (*goal*) to achieve success.

2. Your _____ (*plan*) will not achieve results without more resources.

3. What _____ (*result*) did Gina's persistent lateness have on her job?

Activity 4 Antonyms

Complete these sentences. Use the correct form of the vocabulary word that means the opposite of the word in parentheses.

Example: You need to be persistent when you study _____*complex*_____ (*simple*) math concepts and problems.

1. One last point in my essay was too long, so I had to _____ (*include*) it.

2. Should a _____ (*small*) amount of money be given directly to children?

3. The _____ (*last*) task of the new manager was to modify the schedule.

Activity 5 Use the Vocabulary Words

Complete the paragraph using the correct forms of the vocabulary words from this unit.

Gravity

Why does an apple fall down from a tree and not up? This question helped Sir Isaac Newton

understand the _____ of gravity. Newton was a mathematician in the
                              1.

17th century. He spent _____ time observing movement. His objective was
                                        2.

to explain the forces causing motion. Then he _____ his law of gravity. He
                                                              3.

_____ this law to everything in the universe. The earth's gravity pulls objects
          4.

_____ towards it. When we throw a penny up in the air, it comes back down.
          5.

This is an _____ of gravity. Gravity keeps our feet on the ground.
                        6.

Unit 3

contribute

inevitable proof average intend

extensive interpret

eventually

duration involve comment

preceding

impact relevant

therefore

produce obtain

assume

conflict support

conflict intend assume average obtain
eventually proof **contribute** comment
duration relevant preceding extensive
interpret support impact **inevitable**
proof therefore **involve** produce eventually

Vocabulary Knowledge Rating Chart

How well do you know the words? Use the numbers to rate your knowledge of the vocabulary words. Follow the teacher's directions.

4 = I know the word. I know it well enough to teach it to someone else.
3 = The word is familiar. I think I know what it means.
2 = I have heard the word, but I'm not sure what it means.
1 = I don't know the word at all.

	My rating before instruction	I think the word means	My rating after instruction
conflict			
contribute			
duration			
inevitable			
involve			

Word Meaning Chart

Complete the chart. Follow the teacher's directions.

conflict *(noun)* /KON flikt/   A **conflict** is a serious disagreement between people or events.

EXAMPLES

The _____ in the Middle East has a long history.

Class Example: _____

My Example: I have a **conflict** because the concert is on the same day as _____

contribute *(verb)* /kuhn TRIB yoot/   To **contribute** means to give help or to help something to happen.

EXAMPLES

Spending too much time on the computer may _____ to back or wrist problems.

Class Example: _____

My Example: Our class collected money to **contribute** to _____

duration *(noun)* /doo REY shuhn/   **Duration** is the length of time something continues.

EXAMPLES

The woman in front of me talked to her friend for the _____ of the movie.

Class Example: _____

My Example: For the **duration** of the class, we _____

inevitable *(adjective)* /in EV i tuh buhl/   **Inevitable** tells that something is certain to happen and impossible to avoid.

EXAMPLES

Change is _____. It is a part of life.

Class Example: _____

My Example: The baseball team's loss was **inevitable** because _____

involve *(verb)* /in VOLV/   To **involve** means to include something or someone as a necessary part.

EXAMPLES

The principal wants to _____ parents in the school activities.

Class Example: _____

My Example: Learning vocabulary **involves** _____

Exercise 1   Use the Words

Complete each sentence. Write the correct form of the vocabulary word in the blank space.

1. The class discussion was interesting because all of the students _____ to it.

2. Mrs. Baka had fresh flowers near her bed for the _____ of her hospital stay.

3. What does having your own business _____?

4. After the accident, an increase in our car insurance rates was _____.

5. In the 1800s, there were _____ between farmers and ranchers over the use of land.

Exercise 2   Complete the Sentences

These sentences have been started for you. They are not complete. Complete them with your own words.

1. Instead of donating money, I can contribute _____

_____

_____

2. It is good to involve children in sports because _____

_____

_____

3. The conflict between the neighbors was about _____

_____

_____

4. The coach increased the duration of today's practice because ___

_____

_____

5. For me, an inevitable consequence of not studying is _____

_____

_____

_____

Exercise 3   Words at Work

Circle the best answer to each multiple choice question below. Then write a brief response to the question that follows. Write your answers in complete sentences.

1. Charlotte has a job interview on Monday. She is concerned that a job may cause a conflict with her studies. She takes Saturday classes at a community college. What is a good question for her to ask at the interview?

   (A) Does the job involve travel?
   (B) Does the job involve working on weekends?
   (C) Does the job involve working with customers?

   What does your job involve? What would you like it to involve? _____

   _____

   _____

2. The new owners have analyzed the duration of employee breaks. They are ready to make changes to the break times. How will they modify the duration of the breaks?

   (A) shorten the lunch break
   (B) put a clock on the wall
   (C) ring a bell for all breaks

   What is the duration of your lunch break? Is the time sufficient for you? _____

   _____

   _____

3. Alberto received the Salesperson of the Year Award because he had the highest number of sales in the company. What contributed to Alberto's success?

   (A) his circumstances
   (B) his persistence
   (C) his athletic ability

   What are two other things that contribute to a person's success? _____

   _____

   _____

4. Tanya worked as a waitress while she was a college student. When she graduated, she told her manager that she was hired at Mercy Hospital. Her manager said, "It was inevitable that you would leave us." Why did he say that?

   (A) Her objective was to be a waitress.
   (B) She was happy to graduate.
   (C) Her goal was to become a nurse.

   Is it inevitable that people will change jobs? Why or why not? _____

   _____

   _____

Word Families

Most words are part of a family of words. Study the word families on this page. Then fill in the missing words in the sentences below using the words from this lesson. Use the correct form of each word to complete the sentences.

---

conflict *(noun)*

- **conflict** *(verb)*
  Jim's explanation conflicted with what the teacher told his parents.

- **conflicting** *(adjective)*
  There were conflicting reports about the size of the coming storm.

inevitable *(adjective)*

- **inevitably** *(adverb)*
  Drinking unclean water inevitably leads to illness.

contribute *(verb)*

- **contribution** *(noun)*
  The homeless shelter used Mr. Wu's generous contribution to buy a refrigerator.

involve *(verb)*

- **involvement** *(noun)*
  The mayor announced the involvement of the police in the investigation.

- **involved** *(adjective)*
  It is not good to get involved in other people's arguments.

---

1. The town thanked the government for its _____ of helicopters to the rescue effort.

2. Will you have time to get _____ in the neighborhood clean-up project?

3. I am worried that the needs of my job will _____ with the needs of my family.

4. Babies _____ cry when they are hungry and tired.

5. The _____ of the National Guard in fighting the forest fire prevented it from spreading.

Bill Gates

Bill Gates made significant _____ to computer technology.
                                        6.

He created software programs that made it easier for people to get _____
                                                                                    7.

with computers. He was very successful. _____, people developed
                                                              8.

_____ opinions about Bill Gates. Although he is a powerful businessman,
        9.

he also _____ a lot of money to help people around the world.
                  10.

Human relationships can last a lifetime.

What Do You Think?

Read each question and write a brief answer. Explain your answers in complete sentences.

1. What contributes to the duration of a relationship such as a marriage or friendship?

   _____

   _____

   _____

2. Is conflict among people inevitable or can it be avoided?

   _____

   _____

   _____

3. Can the same things that contribute to a conflict at home contribute to a conflict at work?

   _____

   _____

   _____

Reading Connection

Read the following passage and answer the questions.

The Right to Vote

Voting is a fundamental right of American citizens. In a democracy, voting is a critical way for individuals to express their wishes for local, state, and national governments.

Initially, however, not everybody had the right to vote. Only white males with property could vote when the Constitution was written in 1789.

The voting process is fairer and easier today than it was 220 years ago. The timeline below shows some important events in the history of U.S. voting rights.

1790	Each state determined its own voting laws. There was no national standard for voting. Only white males who owned property could vote.
1850	Most property requirements were removed by 1850.
1870	The 15th Amendment to the Constitution gave former slaves the right to vote. Women could not vote.
1890	Mississippi and other states required voters to take a literacy test. The point was to prevent African Americans, other minorities, and immigrants from voting.
1920	The 19th Amendment gave women the right to vote.
1965	The Voting Rights Act made literacy tests and other barriers illegal.
1971	The 26th Amendment set the minimum voting age at 18.
1993	The Motor Voter Law allowed individuals to register to vote when they applied for a driver's license.
2002	There were major problems counting votes in the 2000 presidential election. The Help America Vote Act was passed to make counting votes easier and more accurate.

1. In what way does an individual's vote contribute to a democracy?

_____

_____

2. What was the duration of the literacy testing that prevented people from voting?

_____

_____

3. What issue was involved in the Help America to Vote Act of 2002?

_____

_____

conflict intend assume average obtain
eventually proof **contribute** comment
duration relevant preceding extensive
interpret support impact **inevitable**
proof therefore **involve** produce eventually

New Word List

☐ conflict

☐ contribute

☐ duration

☐ inevitable

☐ involve

Review Word List

☐ _____

☐ _____

☐ _____

☐ _____

☐ _____

Exercise 7 Writing Connection

Write a brief response to each question. Use words from this lesson or previous lessons in your answer. Write your answers in complete sentences.

In what ways can an individual get involved and contribute to peace in the world? Be specific and give examples.

_____

_____

_____

_____

_____

Some people prefer to ignore or avoid conflict. Other people prefer to face it directly. How do you relate to conflict? Give a specific example.

_____

_____

_____

_____

_____

Exercise 8 Reflection

Think about the words you have studied in this lesson.

1. Which words did you enjoy learning? _____

2. Select one word and imagine where you will use the word. Explain the situation.

_____

_____

3. Which words do you still need help with? _____

4. Return to the Knowledge Rating Chart at the beginning of this lesson. Complete column 3. How have your responses changed?

obtain conflict **preceding** assume average
proof contribute eventually involve comment
duration **relevant** extensive conflict intend
inevitable involve impact interpret **support**
involve obtain **therefore** produce proof

Vocabulary Knowledge Rating Chart

How well do you know the words? Use the numbers to rate your knowledge of the vocabulary words. Follow the teacher's directions.

4 = I know the word. I know it well enough to teach it to someone else.
3 = The word is familiar. I think I know what it means.
2 = I have heard the word, but I'm not sure what it means.
1 = I don't know the word at all.

	My rating before instruction	I think the word means	My rating after instruction
preceding			
proof			
relevant			
support			
therefore			

Word Meaning Chart

Complete the chart. Follow the teacher's directions.

preceding *(adjective)* /pri SEE ding/

Preceding tells that something came before in time, order, or place.

Sales increased 5% over the _____ month's sales.

Class Example: _____

My Example: In the **preceding** election, _____

proof *(noun)* /proof/

Proof means the information or evidence that shows something is true.

Many states require that _____ of car insurance be kept in the car.

Class Example: _____

My Example: I need to show **proof** of my identification when _____

relevant *(adjective)* /REL uh vuhnt/

Relevant tells that something directly concerns the issue being considered.

Understanding the metric system is _____ for medical jobs.

Class Example: _____

My Example: Something I am studying now that is **relevant** to my life is _____

support *(verb)* /suh PORHT/

Support means to provide help so that something can be successful or survive.

A single parent works hard to _____ her family.

Class Example: _____

My Example: Students can **support** their school by _____

therefore *(adverb)* /THAIR fohr/

Therefore means consequently or as a result.

Ms. Kwan's phone number is not listed. _____, it is not in the telephone directory.

Class Example: _____

My Example: I am working on weekends. **Therefore,** _____

Exercise 1 Use the Words

Complete each sentence. Write the correct form of the vocabulary word in the blank space.

1. The U.S. government _____ human rights around the world.

2. The cost of personal computers continues to decrease. _____, more people can afford to buy a home computer.

3. Refer to the map on the _____ page to follow the route that the army traveled.

4. Do you think there is sufficient _____ of global warming?

5. Family medical history is _____ information for a patient's doctor.

Exercise 2 Complete the Sentences

These sentences have been started for you. They are not complete. Complete them with your own words.

1. I can support recycling efforts by _____
   _____
   _____

2. My car broke down. Therefore, _____
   _____
   _____

3. The preceding year was _____ because
   _____
   _____

4. There is proof that exercise _____
   _____
   _____

5. On a resume, relevant information includes _____
   _____
   _____

Words at Work

Circle the best answer to each multiple choice question below. Then write a brief response to the question that follows. Write your answers in complete sentences.

1. Humberto is typing a report for his manager. He notices that on pages 17 and 18 the date of the yearly meeting is different from the date written on the preceding pages. He thinks there is a mistake on pages 17 and 18. Which pages have the correct date?

   (A) pages 15 and 16   **(B)** pages 16 and 17   **(C)** pages 17 and 18

   How can Humberto confirm the correct date on the preceding pages? _____

   _____

   _____

2. The manager told the customer that he could not give a refund without a proof of purchase. What can be used as a proof of purchase?

   (A) a receipt with the item   **(B)** a coupon with the item   **(C)** a price tag from the item
   number on it   listed on it

   What is another reason that a proof of purchase is required? _____

   _____

   _____

3. Ms. Patel is leaving her position as a manager because of a job transfer. Her staff will miss her. They feel that Ms. Patel has supported them. What is an example of Ms. Patel's role?

   (A) She often changed their   **(B)** She told them to clean   **(C)** She listened to their concerns
   work schedules.   up their work stations.   and personal needs.

   What is another way a manager can support her staff? _____

   _____

   _____

4. Rosa had an accident at work last night. She was carrying a box to her car and fell down the steps. Which detail is relevant to her accident and should be included in her report?

   (A) The outside light was   **(B)** It was windy.   **(C)** Rosa was wearing her
   broken.   uniform.

   What is another relevant detail? _____

   _____

   _____

Word Families

Most words are part of a family of words. Study the word families on this page. Then fill in the missing words in the sentences below using the words from this lesson. Use the correct form of each word to complete the sentences.

---

preceding (adjective)

- precede (verb)
  George H. Bush preceded Bill Clinton as president of the United States.

proof (noun)

- prove (verb)
  At the trial, the lawyer proved that his client was innocent.

relevant (adjective)

- relevance (noun)
  The detective recognized the relevance of the information about the robbery.

support (verb)

- support (noun)
  The support of family and friends helped my sister recover from her surgery.
- supporter (noun)
  Mr. Kenton is a big supporter of our city zoo. He contributes a lot of money.

---

1. The doctor explained the _____ of weather to people's moods.

2. Can you _____ that you were home sick yesterday?

3. The candidate invited all her _____ to a victory party after the election.

4. Secret Service agents always _____ the president when he enters a room.

5. The police are more effective when they have the _____ of the community.

Active Seniors

Studies _____ the _____ of social interaction
                    6.   **7.**

to long life. There is evidence to _____ the belief that older people
                                        8.

have fewer health problems if they are active. People also are happier if they have the

_____ of family and friends. Therefore, senior citizens today are
        9.

more active than seniors in _____ generations. They are major
                                    10.

_____ of many groups. They get involved in church, community, and
        11.

political organizations. They are living _____ that friends keep us going!
                                              12.

Homework provides an opportunity for parents to support their children.

Exercise 5 What Do You Think?

Read each question and write a brief answer. Explain your answers in complete sentences.

1. Is the amount of homework a relevant issue for both parents and children? Is it, therefore, an issue that needs to be discussed with teachers?

   _____

   _____

   _____

2. Do people usually support the same political party that the preceding generation of their family supported?

   _____

   _____

   _____

3. Is there sufficient proof to support the view that the world is overpopulated?

   _____

   _____

   _____

Reading Connection

Read the following passage and answer the questions.

The Tallest Living Things on Earth

The United States Capitol building is 288 feet tall. The Statue of Liberty is 305 feet tall. A coast redwood tree can grow to more than 375 feet tall. That is approximately as tall as a 30-floor office building!

Coast redwood trees are the tallest living things on Earth. They can be more than 24 feet wide. They are also among Earth's oldest living things. A coast redwood tree can live for more than 2,000 years.

A redwood tree has bark and wood that are a reddish color. Special chemicals in the bark and leaves fight diseases and insects. The trees also hold a considerable amount of water to help protect them from fire. These natural defenses contribute to the long life of the trees.

The coast redwood comes from a family of trees that lived 144 million years ago during the time of the dinosaurs. The trees grew in North America, Europe, and Asia. Another redwood, the giant sequoia, belongs to the same family.

Today, there is only one place in the world to find coast redwoods. It is along the Pacific coast in northern California and southern Oregon. In this area, the temperatures are not too hot or too cold. The trees like the heavy winter rain. They also like the summer fog that comes in from the ocean.

There used to be more than 2 million acres of redwood forest in California and Oregon. Most of it is gone because of the lumber industry and the development of towns and cities. Now these ancient trees are also in danger from climate change.

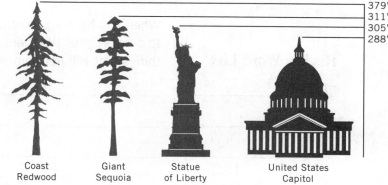

| Coast Redwood | Giant Sequoia | Statue of Liberty | United States Capitol |

379'
311'
305'
288'

1. What natural defenses does the coast redwood have that can support its long life?

   _____

   _____

2. What proof is there that the coast redwood is strong and hardy?

   _____

   _____

3. Do you think efforts to protect redwood trees is a relevant environmental issue? Why?

   _____

   _____

obtain conflict **preceding** assume average
proof contribute eventually involve comment
duration **relevant** extensive conflict intend
inevitable involve impact interpret **support**
involve obtain **therefore** produce proof

New Word List

☐ preceding

☐ proof

☐ relevant

☐ support

☐ therefore

Review Word List

☐ _____

☐ _____

☐ _____

☐ _____

☐ _____

Writing Connection

Write a brief response to each question. Use words from this lesson or previous lessons in your answer. Write your answers in complete sentences.

Imagine you have divided your life into chapters. Describe one of the preceding chapters of your life. How is it different from the current chapter? Are the issues that were relevant to you then still relevant to you now? What are the issues?

_____

_____

_____

_____

_____

When you have a problem, how do you want your family and friends to support you? What are things they can do to help you? What are things that will not help you? Be specific.

_____

_____

_____

_____

_____

Exercise 8 # Reflection

Think about the words you have studied in this lesson.

1. Which words did you enjoy learning? _____

2. Select one word and imagine where you will use the word. Explain the situation.

_____

_____

3. Which words do you still need help with? _____

4. Return to the Knowledge Rating Chart at the beginning of this lesson. Complete column 3. How have your responses changed?

conflict preceding **assume** average obtain

eventually contribute proof comment

duration relevant intend **extensive**

obtain **impact** inevitable support interpret

involve therefore produce **obtain** proof

Vocabulary Knowledge Rating Chart

How well do you know the words? Use the numbers to rate your knowledge of the vocabulary words. Follow the teacher's directions.

4 = I know the word. I know it well enough to teach it to someone else.
3 = The word is familiar. I think I know what it means.
2 = I have heard the word, but I'm not sure what it means.
1 = I don't know the word at all.

	My rating before instruction	I think the word means	My rating after instruction
assume			
eventually			
extensive			
impact			
obtain			

Word Meaning Chart

Complete the chart. Follow the teacher's directions.

assume (verb) /uh SOOM/

To **assume** means to think or believe something is true without having proof.

EXAMPLES

There was a long wait for a table, so we _____ it was a good restaurant.

Class Example: _____

My Example: I **assumed** that Helen was home because _____

eventually (adverb) /ih VEN choo uh lee/

Eventually means what happens in the end after a long time.

EXAMPLES

Walter started as a dishwasher. _____, he became a manager.

Class Example: _____

My Example: The new teacher **eventually** _____

extensive (adjective) /ik STEN siv/

Extensive means large in amount, size, or degree.

EXAMPLES

The tornado caused _____ damage to several homes in one neighborhood.

Class Example: _____

My Example: **Extensive** practice is needed to _____

impact (noun) /im PAKT/

Impact means the effect that an event or situation has on someone or something.

EXAMPLES

The new clinic will have a positive _____ on families with children.

Class Example: _____

My Example: A major oil spill in the ocean has an **impact** on _____

obtain (verb) /uhb TEYN/

To **obtain** means to get something.

EXAMPLES

Where can I _____ a copy of my birth certificate?

Class Example: _____

My Example: I can **obtain** information about store hours by _____

Use the Words

Complete each sentence. Write the correct form of the vocabulary word in the blank space.

1. You will need copies of your recent bank statements to _____ a loan.

2. Higher gas prices can have an _____ on public transportation.

3. There is always _____ television coverage of the Olympic Games.

4. Rodney did exercises to treat his shoulder injury, but he _____ needed surgery.

5. Is it safe to _____ that an emergency vehicle will arrive within 15 minutes of a 911 call?

Exercise 2 Complete the Sentences

These sentences have been started for you. They are not complete. Complete them with your own words.

1. _____ had an impact on our family because _____

_____

_____

2. Because traffic was stopped, we assumed _____

_____

_____

3. After an extensive survey of the students, the school decided

_____

_____

4. When I obtain enough money, _____

_____

_____

5. After waiting for more than 24 hours, I eventually _____

_____

_____

Words at Work

Circle the best answer to each multiple choice question below. Then write a brief response to the question that follows. Write your answers in complete sentences.

1. Ms. Taylor was reading the job applications that she received to fill an office assistant position. She noticed that Jerrod Smith had extensive computer and office experience. Ms. Taylor called Jerrod to tell him that

   (A) he needed more experience.

   (B) the position was filled.

   (C) she wanted to schedule an interview.

   What do you have extensive experience doing? _____

   _____

2. Gloria needs to obtain approval from her manager to change her work schedule next week. What is another reason to obtain her manager's approval?

   (A) to leave work early

   (B) to use her cell phone during lunch

   (C) to answer the telephone

   What do you need to obtain approval or permission to do at work or school?

   _____

   _____

3. S&E Graphics moved to a new site. The move had an impact on all the employees. For Carmen, the impact was positive. Why?

   (A) She can now carpool with a friend.

   (B) It takes 20 minutes longer to get to work.

   (C) The new site is near downtown.

   What decision at school or at work had an impact on you? _____

   _____

   _____

4. On Hector's first day at work, he noticed that many employees obtained their coffee from a coffee pot in the break room. Can Hector assume that the coffee is available to all the employees?

   (A) Yes, because it is in the break room.

   (B) Yes, but he must have his own cup.

   (C) No, because he does not know who pays for it.

   When you are in a new situation, is it safe to assume things? Why or why not?

   _____

   _____

Word Families

Most words are part of a family of words. Study the word families on this page. Then fill in the missing words in the sentences below using the words from this lesson. Use the correct form of each word to complete the sentences.

---

assume *(verb)*

- assumption *(noun)*
  My assumption that the new mayor was going to close the park was incorrect.

eventually *(adverb)*

- eventual *(adjective)*
  The coach may retire, so the school is looking for an eventual replacement.

extensive *(adjective)*

- extensively *(adverb)*
  Lifeguards are trained extensively to rescue people from the water.

impact *(noun)*

- impact *(verb)*
  The closing of Main Street impacted city traffic for weeks.

obtain *(verb)*

- obtainable *(adjective)*
  Most sports equipment is obtainable on the Internet.

---

1. After considerable thought, Norma's _____ decision was to quit smoking.

2. Did the airline strike _____ the travel plans of the wedding guests?

3. Tax and voter registration forms are often _____ at the public library.

4. Dan's _____ about the customer's reaction was based on his previous experience.

5. The scientist _____ analyzed the research before writing her report.

The Telephone

Alexander Graham Bell invented the telephone in 1876. His invention _____
6.

communication. Information became easily _____. Almost every American
7.

would _____ own a telephone. It is safe to _____
8.   9.

that almost no one lives without a phone. Cellular or mobile phones are now used

_____ around the world. One important _____ of
10.   11.

Bell's invention was to make the world a smaller place.

High food costs impact our lives.

Exercise 5   What Do You Think?

Read each question and write a brief answer. Explain your answers in complete sentences.

1. It is possible for higher costs (rent, gas, food, etc.) to eventually have a positive impact?

   _____

   _____

   _____

2. Do you assume that the information that is obtainable on the Internet is true and correct?

   _____

   _____

   _____

3. Do parents have a positive or negative impact when they are extensively involved in their children's lives?

   _____

   _____

   _____

Reading Connection

Read the following passage and answer the questions.

The Story of Chocolate

Chocolate is one of the most popular flavors in the world. People enjoy eating chocolate candy and ice cream, drinking a cup of hot chocolate, or cooking with chocolate. Did you know, however, that chocolate has been around for approximately 3,000 years?

The ancient Olmec and Mayan people lived in Central and South America. They used chocolate to make a drink. The Mayans also had large farms to grow cocoa trees. The trees produce a fruit. The seeds of the fruit are used to make chocolate. The seeds are called cocoa beans.

The powerful Aztecs of central Mexico probably learned about chocolate from the Mayans. The Aztecs used cocoa beans as money. A tamale cost one bean. A turkey hen cost about 100 beans. The Aztecs also forced people to pay a tax of cocoa beans.

The Spaniards arrived in Mexico in the 16th century. Until then, no European had heard of chocolate. The Spaniards discovered that the Aztecs used the cocoa bean to make a chocolate drink. The drink contained chili peppers and other spices. For the Spaniards, the drink was bitter. They replaced the chili peppers with vanilla and added honey to sweeten it.

In 1528, the conquistador Hernando Cortez returned to Spain with cocoa beans. Drinking chocolate soon became popular in Europe. Europeans believed chocolate had special qualities to keep them healthy.

Chocolate candy, however, did not exist until the middle of the 19th century. Today, chocolate is a $4 billion industry in the United States. The average American consumes approximately 12 pounds of chocolate each year.

1. Imagine you live in the Aztec culture. What could you obtain with cocoa beans? How else would chocolate be a part of your life?

   _____

   _____

2. What impact did chocolate have on Europe when it was first introduced by the Spanish?

   _____

   _____

3. Is it fair to assume that chocolate has an extensive impact on the United States today? Explain your answer.

   _____

   _____

conflict preceding **assume** average obtain
eventually contribute proof comment
duration relevant intend **extensive**
obtain **impact** inevitable support interpret
involve therefore produce **obtain** proof

New Word List

☐ assume

☐ eventually

☐ extensive

☐ impact

☐ obtain

Review Word List

☐ _____

☐ _____

☐ _____

☐ _____

☐ _____

Exercise 7 # Writing Connection

Write a brief response to each question. Use words from this lesson or previous lessons in your answer. Write your answers in complete sentences.

The telephone and computer are two inventions that have had an extensive impact on our lives. Name one other invention and describe how it has extensively impacted our lives.

_____

_____

_____

_____

_____

"The more valuable a thing is, the more difficult it is to obtain." Do you agree with the preceding statement? Explain your answer with specific examples.

_____

_____

_____

_____

_____

Exercise 8 # Reflection

Think about the words you have studied in this lesson.

1. Which words did you enjoy learning? _____

2. Select one word and imagine where you will use the word. Explain the situation.

_____

_____

3. Which words do you still need help with? _____

4. Return to the Knowledge Rating Chart at the beginning of this lesson. Complete column 3. How have your responses changed?

conflict preceding assume **average** obtain
comment contribute inevitable eventually
duration relevant **intend** extensive involve
proof inevitable support impact **interpret**
involve **produce** therefore obtain proof

Vocabulary Knowledge Rating Chart

How well do you know the words? Use the numbers to rate your knowledge of the vocabulary words. Follow the teacher's directions.

4 = I know the word. I know it well enough to teach it to someone else.
3 = The word is familiar. I think I know what it means.
2 = I have heard the word, but I'm not sure what it means.
1 = I don't know the word at all.

	My rating before instruction	I think the word means	My rating after instruction
average			
comment			
intend			
interpret			
produce			

Word Meaning Chart

Complete the chart. Follow the teacher's directions.

average *(adjective)* /AV er ij/ — **Average** means possessing qualities that are common to most people or things.

EXAMPLES

The _____ man is about 69.2 inches tall.

Class Example: _____

My Example: In an **average** classroom, you will find _____

---

comment *(noun)* /KOM ent/ — A **comment** is a spoken or written expression of an opinion or idea.

EXAMPLES

Based on the customers' _____, the store hours were extended.

Class Example: _____

My Example: After the game, the coach made **comments** about _____

---

intend *(verb)* /in TEND/ — To **intend** is to plan to do something.

EXAMPLES

On his first day of vacation, Greg _____ to sleep late.

Class Example: _____

My Example: In order to get in shape, Sayed **intends** to _____

---

interpret *(verb)* /in TUR prit/ — To **interpret** is to explain or decide the meaning of something.

EXAMPLES

Judges do not make laws. They _____ them.

Class Example: _____

My Example: On a test, students are asked to **interpret** _____

---

produce *(verb)* /pruh DOOS/ — To **produce** is to grow or make something.

EXAMPLES

White blood cells _____ antibodies to fight infection in the body.

Class Example: _____

My Example: I wish the auto industry could **produce** a car that _____

Use the Words

Complete each sentence. Write the correct form of the vocabulary word in the blank space.

1. Raisa _____ to read two chapters before watching television.

2. Did you know that one barrel of crude oil _____ approximately 20 gallons of gasoline?

3. Scientists _____ images sent back to Earth from satellite cameras.

4. Beth was pleased to read the teacher's _____ written on her homework.

5. The U.S. Census states that the _____ American family has 1.82 children.

Exercise 2 Complete the Sentences

These sentences have been started for you. They are not complete. Complete them with your own words.

1. An interesting comment I heard today about _____ was _____

_____

_____

2. For me, an average morning includes _____

_____

_____

3. Good communication between parents and children produces _____

_____

_____

4. Another person's silence can be interpreted to mean _____

_____

_____

_____

5. By the end of the year, I intend to _____

_____

_____

Words at Work

Circle the best answer to each multiple choice question below. Then write a brief response to the question that follows. Write your answers in complete sentences.

1. The bus company intends to increase fares by the end of the year. Marcie wants to make some comments about the increase. She writes a letter to the bus company. What is one of Marcie's comments?

   (A) The increase is unfair to bus riders.
   (B) She likes the color of the buses.
   (C) She does not take the bus on Sunday.

   What is another comment Marcie could make to support her opinion? _____

   _____

2. On an average work day, Kimo travels to different customers' homes to install ceiling fans and light fixtures. Sometimes he gets so busy that he forgets to eat lunch. However, he never forgets to call his wife. Today was not an average work day. Why not?

   (A) He did not have lunch.
   (B) He called his wife.
   (C) He worked only in one home.

   Was today an average day for you? Why or why not? _____

   _____

3. Diego works for a company that produces electrical equipment. It is a good company to work for. He intends to stay with the company and hopes eventually to become a manager. What can you assume Diego will do?

   (A) look for another job
   (B) work hard and learn as much as he can
   (C) take an extra day off each month

   What else can Diego do to achieve his goal? _____

   _____

4. Alonzo made a funny comment at a staff meeting. Everyone except Jill laughed. What was the reason Jill did not laugh?

   (A) She interpreted his comment to be funny.
   (B) She did not interpret his comment.
   (C) She did not interpret his comment to be funny.

   Why do people interpret comments differently? _____

   _____

   _____

Word Families

Most words are part of a family of words. Study the word families on this page. Then fill in the missing words in the sentences below using the words from this lesson. Use the correct form of each word to complete the sentences.

---

average *(adjective)*

- average *(noun)*
  Today's temperature was above average.

comment *(noun)*

- comment *(verb)*
  The basketball players were asked to comment on the final game of the season.

interpret *(verb)*

- interpretation *(noun)*
  A poem can have different interpretations depending on the reader.
- interpreter *(noun)*
  The Chinese tourists obtained an interpreter for the museum tour.

produce *(verb)*

- producer *(noun)*
  California is a major producer of wine.
- product *(noun)*
  Companies test their products before selling them.
- production *(noun)*
  The production of sweat is intended to cool the body.
- productive *(adjective)*
  We had a productive meeting because we determined the new schedule.

---

1. The mayor refused to _____ on the city workers' strike.

2. On _____, we go out to dinner about twice a month.

3. What is your _____ of the neighbor's strange behavior?

4. Cheese, butter, and milk are all dairy _____.

5. Agnes is more _____ in the morning than in the afternoon.

Making Movies

A movie is a _____ of the film industry. While a movie is in
                    6.

_____, many decisions need to be made. The _____
        7.   **8.**

is responsible for quite a few of the decisions. She or he helps determine which

_____ of the story that the movie will tell. The producer hopes that the
        9.

_____ movie-goer will enjoy the movie and, therefore, make
        10.

positive _____ about it.
              11.

Artists use colors and shapes to express their ideas to other people.

Exercise 5 What Do You Think?

Read each question and write a brief answer. Explain your answers in complete sentences.

1. Is art intended for the average person?

_____

_____

_____

2. Do companies ever intend to produce products of poor quality?

_____

_____

_____

3. Are comments from an average person as important as comments from a celebrity?

_____

_____

_____

Reading Connection

Read the following passage and answer the questions.

The Trail of Tears

In the early 1800s, several Native American tribes lived in the Southeastern states. One tribe, the Cherokee, lived mostly in Georgia. The Cherokee lived on land that was good for growing cotton. Georgia's economy relied heavily on this critical crop. Consequently, the state of Georgia put pressure on the U.S. government to force the Cherokee to leave.

In 1830, Congress approved the Indian Removal Act. This law required Native American tribes east of the Mississippi River to give up their land. They had to move to the new Indian Territory west of the Mississippi. Today this area is in the state of Oklahoma.

Some Native American tribes did give up their land and move to the new area. However, the Cherokee refused to leave their homeland.

In 1838, President Martin Van Buren determined that the Cherokee had to move. He ordered the U.S. Army to force the Cherokee people to leave their homes. The soldiers removed more than 15,000 Cherokees from their land. They were forced to walk hundreds of miles in the winter to the new territory. It took them five months.

John G. Burnett was one of the soldiers. He eventually wrote a letter in 1890 to his children to describe the event. He wrote: "I saw helpless Cherokees arrested and dragged from their homes…. I saw them loaded like cattle or sheep into wagons…. Many of these helpless people did not have blankets…." He also noticed that many of them were barefoot.

Approximately 4,000 Cherokee people died during the march. This forced march became known as the Trail of Tears.

1. What did Georgia produce that was so important to the economy of the South?

_____

_____

_____

2. How do Private Burnett's comments provide proof that a tragic outcome was inevitable?

_____

_____

_____

3. The Trail of Tears is recognized as a critical event in Cherokee history. How do you interpret this event in U.S. history?

_____

_____

_____

conflict preceding assume **average** obtain **comment** contribute inevitable eventually duration relevant **intend** extensive involve proof inevitable support impact **interpret** involve **produce** therefore obtain proof

New Word List

☐ average

☐ comment

☐ intend

☐ interpret

☐ produce

Review Word List

☐ _____

☐ _____

☐ _____

☐ _____

☐ _____

Exercise 7 Writing Connection

Write a brief response to each question. Use words from this lesson or previous lessons in your answer. Write your answers in complete sentences.

How do you interpret the term "average parent"? Explain some of the qualities of an average parent.

_____

_____

_____

_____

_____

Consider a time in your life when you had a different interpretation of an experience than someone else. It could be a movie, a song, a situation, or some other event. Explain how two people can interpret the same experience differently. What influences produce different interpretations?

_____

_____

_____

_____

_____

Exercise 8 Reflection

Think about the words you have studied in this lesson.

1. Which words did you enjoy learning? _____

2. Select one word and imagine where you will use the word. Explain the situation.

_____

_____

3. Which words do you still need help with? _____

4. Return to the Knowledge Rating Chart at the beginning of this lesson. Complete column 3. How have your responses changed?

Activity 1 Ask Questions

Look at the picture. Imagine you have the opportunity to ask the candidate several questions before you vote. Write at least five questions you want to ask the candidate. Use one or more of the vocabulary words you have studied in this unit in each question. <u>Underline</u> each vocabulary word you use. You may also use words from previous units. Some of your questions can begin with *Who*, *What*, *When*, *Where*, *Why* or *How*.

Example: How do you <u>intend</u> to <u>support</u> education?

_____

_____

_____

_____

_____

_____

_____

_____

_____

_____

_____

_____

WORD BANK

ASSUME
AVERAGE
COMMENT
CONFLICT
CONTRIBUTE
DURATION
EVENTUALLY
EXTENSIVE
IMPACT
INEVITABLE
INTEND
INTERPRET
INVOLVE
OBTAIN
PRECEDING
PRODUCE
PROOF
RELEVANT
SUPPORT
THEREFORE

Activity 2 Puzzle

ACROSS

1. Did Shayla _____ to get concert tickets for us?
3. What is the _____ of the budget cut on you?
6. The questions were not _____ to the topic.
7. The lights are on inside, so I _____ Tom is home.
9. I'm not sure how to _____ these math symbols.
10. You'll need to _____ a note from your doctor.
14. Our summer garden will _____ beans and corn.
15. The _____ search for the boy lasted two days.
17. No one is perfect. Mistakes are _____.
18. What caused the _____ between the two teams?

DOWN

2. After a long delay, the plane _____ took off.
4. "Senator, would you like to make a _____?"
5. Do cell phones _____ to traffic accidents?
7. An _____ night's sleep is 7.5 hours.
8. Anna will _____ her brother until he finds a job.
11. A green card is _____ of U.S. residency.
12. Luis fell asleep. _____, he was late for work.
13. The baby slept for the _____ of the flight.
14. Jenna's _____ two paychecks had mistakes.
16. The job will _____ speaking with customers.

Activity 3 Synonyms

Complete these sentences. Use the correct form of the vocabulary word that means the same as the word or words in parentheses.

Example: Did you know that the liver ___produces___ (*makes*) cholesterol?

1. After several years, Rudy eventually _____ (*got*) his real estate license.

2. What was the impact of the _____ (*serious disagreement*) at work?

3. The union supported the workers for the _____ (*length*) of the strike.

Activity 4 Antonyms

Complete these sentences. Use the correct form of the vocabulary word that means the opposite of the word or words in parentheses.

Example: The ___preceding___ (*following*) comments are not relevant to this discussion.

1. Dr. Baker _____ (*took*) time, support, and money to the project.

2. It was an _____ (*special*) day. Therefore, nothing unusual happened.

3. Why did he assume Ben had _____ (*a little*) experience with computers?

Activity 5 Use the Vocabulary Words

Complete the paragraph with correct forms of the vocabulary words from this unit.

The Civil War

The Civil War began as a _____ between the North and the South.
                                1.

The South needed slaves to _____ cotton and other crops. The North
                                2.

did not _____ slavery and _____ to make it illegal
              3.   4.

_____. When the Southern states separated from the U.S., war was
        5.

_____. President Abraham Lincoln was determined to preserve the unity of
        6.

the country. _____, he _____ permission from Congress
                      7.   8.

to go to war.

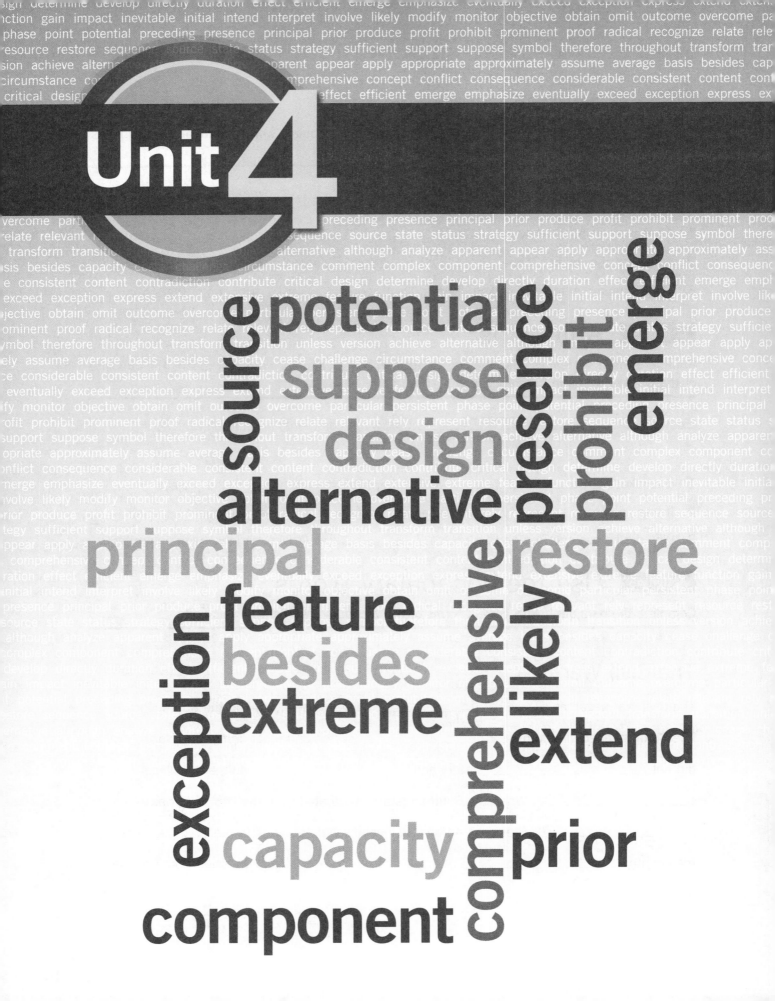

alternative comprehensive besides emerge
component likely extreme **capacity** exception
potential **extend** alternative presence design
prior feature extreme source component **likely**
presence prohibit **restore** principal suppose

Vocabulary Knowledge Rating Chart

How well do you know the words? Use the numbers to rate your knowledge of the vocabulary words. Follow the teacher's directions.

4 = I know the word. I know it well enough to teach it to someone else.
3 = The word is familiar. I think I know what it means.
2 = I have heard the word, but I'm not sure what it means.
1 = I don't know the word at all.

	My rating before instruction	I think the word means	My rating after instruction
alternative			
capacity			
extend			
likely			
restore			

Word Meaning Chart

Complete the chart. Follow the teacher's directions.

alternative *(adjective)* /awl TUR nuh tiv/

Alternative means that something can be used in place of another thing.

EXAMPLES

The road was closed, so we used an _____ route to get downtown.

Class Example: _____

My Example: The library is a good place to study. An **alternative** place is _____

capacity *(noun)* /kuh PAS i tee/

Capacity is the ability to do, experience, or contain something.

EXAMPLES

The small hospital does not have the _____ to treat critically injured people.

Class Example: _____

My Example: My cell phone has the **capacity** to _____

extend *(verb)* /ik STEND/

To **extend** means to include, continue, reach, or make something larger or longer.

EXAMPLES

The United States _____ from the Pacific Ocean to the Atlantic Ocean.

Class Example: _____

My Example: I wish our school would **extend** _____

likely *(adjective)* /LAHYK lee/

Likely means that something will probably happen or is almost certain.

EXAMPLES

It is _____ that her recovery from surgery will involve physical therapy.

Class Example: _____

My Example: One **likely** effect of waking up late is _____

restore *(verb)* /ri STOHR/

To **restore** means to bring something back to its previous condition or situation.

EXAMPLES

After the storm, it took two days for the power company to _____ the electricity.

Class Example: _____

My Example: The police arrived to **restore** order after the _____

Exercise 1 Use the Words

Complete each sentence. Write the correct form of the vocabulary word in the blank space.

1. Unless you apply your new computer skills, you are _____ to forget them.

2. "The objective," said the senator, "is to _____ health benefits to all Americans."

3. The coach develops _____ strategies to successfully play against different teams.

4. Did the historical society obtain approval to _____ the old library?

5. The owners of the shoe factory determined that it had the _____ to increase production by 10%.

Exercise 2 Complete the Sentences

These sentences have been started for you. They are not complete. Complete them with your own words.

1. I am most likely to feel motivated when _____

_____

_____

2. When I get stressed, I restore my calm by _____

_____

_____

3. I would like to develop the capacity to _____

_____

_____

4. If it rains, our alternative plan is to _____

_____

_____

5. We were able to extend the time on the parking meter, so _____

_____

_____

Words at Work

Circle the best answer to each multiple choice question below. Then write a brief response to the question that follows. Write your answers in complete sentences.

1. The building management extended the contract for Frank's Food Truck for another year. What can the building employees expect of Frank's Food Truck?

   (A) It will continue to sell food.

   (B) It will sell food for six more months.

   (C) It will be replaced soon.

   What is another type of contract that a person or company can extend? _____

   _____

   _____

2. The new owners of the Pizza Palace want to increase the restaurant's capacity to serve more customers. What can the owners do?

   (A) obtain more menus and signs

   (B) get new uniforms for the employees

   (C) obtain another oven and more workers

   What else can the Pizza Palace owners do to increase its capacity? _____

   _____

   _____

3. Precision Paper Factory wants to increase production. They are offering employees alternative ways to work overtime. What is one of the ways?

   (A) Employees can work after their shifts.

   (B) Employees can change shifts.

   (C) Employees can produce more during their shifts.

   What is another alternative way to work overtime? _____

   _____

   _____

4. As a new employee, Glenda cannot start working until she gets a physical from her doctor and turns in the required forms. The doctor's office tells her she is not likely to obtain an appointment this week. When is Glenda likely to start working?

   (A) sometime this week

   (B) sometime next week

   (C) the day after tomorrow

   What are some other likely things a new employee will have to do before starting work?

   _____

   _____

Word Families

Most words are part of a family of words. Study the word families on this page. Then fill in the missing words in the sentences below using the words from this lesson. Use the correct form of each word to complete the sentences.

---

alternative *(adjective)*

- alternative *(noun)*
  Honey is a healthy alternative to white sugar.

extend *(verb)*

- extension *(noun)*
  Earl got an extension on his taxes. They are now due September 15.

restore *(verb)*

- restoration *(noun)*
  The restoration of the train station took almost a year.

capacity *(noun)*

- capable *(adjective)*
  My camera is capable of taking photographs and filming videos.

- capability *(noun)*
  Pam has the capability to be a good reporter because she is persistent.

likely *(adjective)*

- likelihood *(noun)*
  Mr. Kim emphasized the likelihood that the store would extend its hours.

- likely *(adverb)*
  The new park will most likely open next spring.

---

1. Lorna is quite _____ of representing our department at the meeting.

2. What is the _____ that the final phase of the project will end next month?

3. We are relying on the mayor to support our proposal for an _____ to the bike path.

4. The _____ to cutting a position is to reduce everyone's hours.

5. The museum is known for its _____ of old photographs.

The Tongue

The tongue is a critical organ. It gives us the _____ to speak. It is also
                                                    6.
_____ of determining tastes. The tongue is made up of muscles, so it
        7.
can _____ itself to lick things, such as an envelope. The tongue has the
         8.
_____ to _____ itself and quickly heal minor cuts
        9.   **10.**
and burns. The _____ that a tongue needs stitches is rare. Often we are
                      11.
_____ to forget how essential the tongue is.
        12.

The right tools are only part of what gives a person the capacity to make furniture.

Exercise 5 What Do You Think?

Read each question and write a brief answer. Explain your answers in complete sentences.

1. Which alternative would you likely choose to complete a project: extend the deadline or increase your capacity to do the work?

   _____

   _____

   _____

2. What is the likelihood that a person can restore his or her reputation once it has been considerably damaged?

   _____

   _____

   _____

3. Would you support extending the school year as an alternative way to improve student achievement?

   _____

   _____

Reading Connection

Read the following passage and answer the questions.

The Democratic Party

The United States has a two-party political system. In this system, two political parties control the political process. The two major parties are the Democratic Party and the Republican Party. The parties represent different points of view about the way the country should operate. The parties have long histories, and they have helped to determine the direction of the country. Below are some relevant facts about the Democratic Party. You will read about the Republican Party in Lesson 17.

Thomas Jefferson started the Democratic Party in the 1790s. Initially, it was called the Democratic-Republican Party. The name changed to the Democratic Party in 1828.

A donkey is the symbol of the party. It started in 1828 when Andrew Jackson ran for president. Someone called him a "jackass" to mean that he was foolish. However, Jackson thought a donkey represented a persistent animal. Therefore, he used the donkey to symbolize his campaign.

The Democratic Party has often been called "the party of the common man." Many immigrants came to the U.S. in the 19th century. They lived mainly in industrial cities and began to form the base of the party. The Democrats became the major party in many cities and urban areas. The party is still popular among immigrants and working people.

Democrats believe that government should assist people in time of need. Franklin D. Roosevelt reinforced that idea when he was the Democratic president during the Great Depression in the 1930s. Roosevelt started programs that put people to work building highways and dams. He also started the Social Security program.

Democratic president Harry S. Truman desegregated the Army in 1948 and president Lyndon B. Johnson started Medicare and signed the 1964 Civil Rights Act. Other important Democratic presidents include John F. Kennedy, Bill Clinton, and Barack Obama.

1. Why does the Democratic Party have the capacity to attract immigrants and working people?

_____

_____

2. As president during the Great Depression, Franklin Roosevelt restored jobs. What else did he achieve as president?

_____

_____

3. Is it likely the Democratic Party would support a bill to extend the rights of workers? Why?

_____

_____

alternative comprehensive besides emerge
component likely extreme **capacity** exception
potential **extend** alternative presence design
prior feature extreme source component **likely**
presence prohibit **restore** principal suppose

New Word List

☐ alternative

☐ capacity

☐ extend

☐ likely

☐ restore

Review Word List

☐ _____

☐ _____

☐ _____

☐ _____

☐ _____

Writing Connection

Write a brief response to each question. Use words from this lesson or previous lessons in your answer. Write your answers in complete sentences.

Think of someone whose influence has extended beyond his or her country. What impact has that person had? Identify the person and explain why his or her influence extends across boundaries or generations.

_____

_____

_____

_____

_____

What is the objective of having an alternative plan? When do you need to have an alternative plan? Describe the circumstances of a time you used an alternative plan. What was the outcome?

_____

_____

_____

_____

_____

Reflection

Think about the words you have studied in this lesson.

1. Which words did you enjoy learning? _____

2. Select one word and imagine where you will use the word. Explain the situation.

_____

_____

3. Which words do you still need help with? _____

4. Return to the Knowledge Rating Chart at the beginning of this lesson. Complete column 3. How have your responses changed?

alternative comprehensive **besides** emerge
component extreme capacity exception
potential suppose presence extend **design**
likely **feature** extreme source component
prior prohibit restore **principal** suppose

Vocabulary Knowledge Rating Chart

How well do you know the words? Use the numbers to rate your knowledge of the vocabulary words. Follow the teacher's directions.

4 = I know the word. I know it well enough to teach it to someone else.
3 = The word is familiar. I think I know what it means.
2 = I have heard the word, but I'm not sure what it means.
1 = I don't know the word at all.

	My rating before instruction	I think the word means	My rating after instruction
besides			
component			
design			
feature			
principal			

Word Meaning Chart

Complete the chart. Follow the teacher's directions.

besides *(preposition and adverb)* /bih SAHYDZ/ — **Besides** means in addition to.

EXAMPLES

_____ George Washington, President's Day also honors Abraham Lincoln.

Class Example: _____

My Example: **Besides** going to school, I _____

component *(noun)* /kuhm POH nuhnt/ — A **component** is one of several parts of something.

EXAMPLES

The keyboard is one _____ of my computer system.

Class Example: _____

My Example: Hard work is one **component** of success. Another component is _____

design *(verb)* /dih ZAHYN/ — To **design** means to create or develop something.

EXAMPLES

Companies _____ computers for home and business use.

Class Example: _____

My Example: Teachers **design** _____

feature *(noun)* /FEE cher/ — A **feature** is an important or interesting part of something.

EXAMPLES

The circular staircase is a unique _____ of the old house.

Class Example: _____

My Example: One optional **feature** on a car is _____

principal *(adjective)* /PRIN suh puhl/ — **Principal** means that something is the most important.

EXAMPLES

The rain was the _____ cause of the traffic problems this evening.

Class Example: _____

My Example: My **principal** reason for coming to school is _____

Exercise 1   Use the Words

Complete each sentence. Write the correct form of the vocabulary word in the blank space.

1. Henry Ford _____ the assembly line factory to produce cars quickly and cheaply.

2. A critical _____ of the mayor's crime-prevention strategy is to involve neighborhoods and businesses.

3. Mr. Tan's experience is appropriate for the job. He has excellent references

   _____ .

4. Did General Williams achieve his _____ objective?

5. The employees were trained to explain the most useful _____ of each product to their customers.

Exercise 2   Complete the Sentences

These sentences have been started for you. They are not complete. Complete them with your own words.

1. One component of a healthy diet is _____

   _____

   _____

2. I wish someone would design _____

   _____

   _____

3. One feature of my city that I enjoy is _____

   _____

   _____

4. The apartment is too small. Besides, _____

   _____

   _____

5. In my opinion, the principal issue that challenges the average

   American is _____

   _____

Words at Work

Circle the best answer to each multiple choice question below. Then write a brief response to the question that follows. Write your answers in complete sentences.

1. Shirley works for G & S Electronics. The company wants Shirley to be part of a team that will design an orientation program for new employees. Why does the company want Shirley's help?

   (A) She is never late for work.
   (B) She has been with the company for 30 years.
   (C) She works the day shift.

   Why does the team need to design an orientation program? _____

   _____

2. Troy is a new employee. He commented to his co-worker, "The principal reason I took this job is for the benefits. Although this job is farther from my home, it provides partial health benefits." What can you assume about Troy's previous job?

   (A) It provided benefits.
   (B) It did not provide benefits.
   (C) It was farther from Troy's home.

   What is another principal reason that people accept jobs? _____

   _____

3. Cynthia is considerably happier with her new job than her previous one. Besides the convenient location, what also likely contributes to Cynthia's job satisfaction?

   (A) the support of her manager
   (B) her reliance on computers
   (C) persistent phone calls

   Besides Cynthia's reason, what is another reason for job satisfaction? _____

   _____

   _____

4. Home Designs has a large number of employees, so it has the capacity to offer group rates for insurance. One feature of the insurance plan that the employees like is

   (A) the option to add family members.
   (B) the need to show proof of employment for at least one year.
   (C) the requirement to pay the total amount of the premium.

   What is another feature that you would like from an insurance plan? _____

   _____

   _____

Exercise 4 Word Families

Most words are part of a family of words. Study the word families on this page. Then fill in the missing words in the sentences below using the words from this lesson. Use the correct form of each word to complete the sentences.

---

design *(verb)*

- design *(noun)*
  The new design of the suitcases makes them lighter and easier to use.

- designer *(noun)*
  Clothing designers need to be creative people.

principal *(adjective)*

- principally *(adverb)*
  These chairs were designed principally for people with back problems.

- principal *(noun)*
  Unless the principal is ill, she will speak at the graduation ceremony.

feature *(noun)*

- feature *(verb)*
  The new gym features a sauna and a hot tub.

---

1. Next month, the museum will _____ the work of approximately 20 local artists.

2. Do car _____ also need to be engineers?

3. The detective asked Millie to describe the physical _____ of the man she saw.

4. Wilson was asked to modify his _____ for the new cafeteria.

5. Although baking soda is _____ used for baking, it is also good for cleaning.

The White House

George Washington, the first U.S. president, determined that a "President's House" was needed.

Although this building _____ would be a private home, it would also
      6.

include an office for the president. In 1792, James Hoban, an Irish _____,
      7.

created a _____ that _____ four tall pillars
   8.   **9.**

in the front of the building. His design was selected. Today, the White House is a

_____ symbol of the United States.
   10.

Theme parks have many features that are entertaining.

What Do You Think?

Read each question and write a brief answer. Explain your answers in complete sentences.

1. Is a theme park designed principally for children or adults?

_____

_____

_____

2. Will computers eventually be the principal component of the educational system?

_____

_____

_____

3. Besides good health, is money a significant feature of a happy life?

_____

_____

_____

Reading Connection

Read the following passage and answer the questions.

The Human Heart

The design of the heart is simple but amazing. It is a hollow muscle in the middle of the chest. It is not very big—approximately the size of a person's fist. However, its job is enormous. The heart pumps blood to all parts of the body.

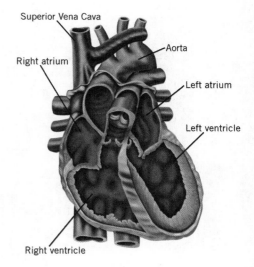

The heart is divided into four sections called chambers. There are two chambers on the right side and two on the left.

The left side receives blood from the lungs where it gets oxygen. Then the heart pumps this oxygen-rich blood through the *aorta* directly to all parts of the body. A series of valves controls the flow of blood into and out of the chambers.

The blood delivers the oxygen to cells in the body. Then the blood flows back to the right side of the heart through the blood vessel called the *vena cava*. The heart pumps this blood to the lungs, where it obtains a new supply of oxygen. Then the cycle is repeated.

Each heart beat means that blood is being pumped out to the body. The heart normally beats between 60 and 80 times per minute. However, during exercise, the heart can beat 200 times a minute. Regular exercise helps strengthen the heart muscle. A person needs a strong heart because, on average, it will beat approximately 2.5 billion times in a lifetime!

1. What is the heart designed to do?

_____

_____

_____

2. What are four of the principal components of the heart? What are other components?

_____

_____

_____

3. Besides exercise, what else contributes to a healthy heart?

_____

_____

_____

alternative comprehensive **besides** emerge
component extreme capacity exception
potential suppose presence extend **design**
likely **feature** extreme source component
prior prohibit restore **principal** suppose

New Word List

☐ besides

☐ component

☐ design

☐ feature

☐ principal

Review Word List

☐ _____

☐ _____

☐ _____

☐ _____

☐ _____

Exercise 7 # Writing Connection

Write a brief response to each question. Use words from this lesson or previous lessons in your answer. Write your answers in complete sentences.

Imagine you have the opportunity to design your own home. Think about the size of your house and the features it will have. Describe two or three of the principal features of your house.

_____

_____

_____

_____

_____

Besides the United States, is there another place you would like to live? Why or why not? What is your principal reason? Be specific.

_____

_____

_____

_____

_____

Exercise 8 # Reflection

Think about the words you have studied in this lesson.

1. Which words did you enjoy learning? _____

2. Select one word and imagine where you will use the word. Explain the situation.

_____

_____

3. Which words do you still need help with? _____

4. Return to the Knowledge Rating Chart at the beginning of this lesson. Complete column 3. How have your responses changed?

alternative **comprehensive** presence
component extreme capacity **exception**
potential emerge besides extend design
feature extreme **source** component likely
prior prohibit restore principal **suppose**

Vocabulary Knowledge Rating Chart

How well do you know the words? Use the numbers to rate your knowledge of the vocabulary words. Follow the teacher's directions.

4 = I know the word. I know it well enough to teach it to someone else.
3 = The word is familiar. I think I know what it means.
2 = I have heard the word, but I'm not sure what it means.
1 = I don't know the word at all.

	My rating before instruction	I think the word means	My rating after instruction
comprehensive			
exception			
potential			
source			
suppose			

Word Meaning Chart

Complete the chart. Follow the teacher's directions.

comprehensive *(adjective)* /kom pri HEN siv/
Comprehensive means that something is complete and includes all that is necessary.

EXAMPLES

New soldiers are given _____ physical examinations to determine their health and physical condition.

Class Example: _____

My Example: A job that requires **comprehensive** training is _____

exception *(noun)* /ik SEP shuhn/
Exception means the person or thing that is not included or does not follow a rule.

EXAMPLES

With the _____ of emergency vehicles, there is no parking in the red zone.

Class Example: _____

My Example: Rosalie asked the teacher to make an **exception** and _____

potential *(noun)* /puh TEN shuhl/
Potential means the possibility that something will develop or happen in the future.

EXAMPLES

The dedicated new volunteers have the _____ to be excellent teacher aides.

Class Example: _____

My Example: When children are left alone, there is the **potential** for _____

source *(noun)* /sohrs/
The word **source** tells where something comes from.

EXAMPLES

A theme park is a _____ of fun and excitement.

Class Example: _____

My Example: A **source** of joy for me is _____

suppose *(verb)* /suh POHZ/
To **suppose** is to think or believe something is probably true.

EXAMPLES

Do you _____ the school football team will make it to the playoffs this year?

Class Example: _____

My Example: I **suppose** that the teacher _____

Exercise 1 Use the Words

Complete each sentence. Write the correct form of the vocabulary word in the blank space.

1. Arnold is careful about his diet, and tonight was no _____.
   He ordered grilled fish and a salad.

2. The Internet it is not always an accurate _____ of information.

3. The _____ television program about baseball covered 150 years of the sport's history.

4. There is no reason to _____ that the train will be late.

5. Does the storm have the _____ to become a powerful hurricane?

Exercise 2 Complete the Sentences

These sentences have been started for you. They are not complete. Complete them with your own words.

1. A source of pride for the average American is _____

   _____

   _____

2. This year the team has the potential to be champions because _____

   _____

   _____

3. I need to give a comprehensive explanation when _____

   _____

   _____

4. I suppose the movie is good because _____

   _____

   _____

5. "You are not an exception to the rule," said his mother.

   "You _____

   _____

   _____

Words at Work

Circle the best answer to each multiple choice question below. Then write a brief response to the question that follows. Write your answers in complete sentences.

1. Margot's mother returned from the clinic. Her mother told her that without exception, everyone at the clinic was kind and helpful. What did she mean?

    (A) The nurse was not nice.   **(B)** Most people were nice.   **(C)** Everybody was nice.

    What is an experience you had when everyone, without exception, was nice to you? _____

    _____

    _____

2. The company owner asked Mr. Cho for his opinion about two job applicants. Mr. Cho said, "They are young and have little experience. However, I think they have potential." What is the owner likely to do?

    (A) She will not hire them.   **(B)** She will hire them on a   **(C)** She will hire them on a
    test or trial basis.   permanent basis.

    Why does an employer look for workers who have potential? _____

    _____

    _____

3. The mall has an exhibit called "American First Ladies: A Comprehensive Look Through the Years." What can you expect to see when you visit the exhibit?

    (A) pictures of the most   **(B)** pictures of recent first   **(C)** pictures of all first ladies
    important first ladies   ladies

    What would a comprehensive exhibit about first ladies allow you to compare? _____

    _____

    _____

4. Luther is a reporter for a newspaper. He writes about sports, so he often attends games and talks to players to get reliable information about effective game strategies. What other sources do you suppose Luther uses?

    (A) coaches and managers   **(B)** taxi drivers and fans   **(C)** hot dog vendors and
    ticket sellers

    What is a source you use for reliable information about school or work? _____

    _____

    _____

Word Families

Most words are part of a family of words. Study the word families on this page. Then fill in the missing words in the sentences below using the words from this lesson. Use the correct form of each word to complete the sentences.

comprehensive (*adjective*)	**exception** (*noun*)
• comprehensively (*adverb*) The teacher comprehensively explained the causes of the Civil War.	• except (*preposition, conjunction*) The beauty salon is open every day except Monday.
potential (*noun*)	**suppose** (*verb*)
• potential (*adjective*) My mechanic told me there may be a potential problem with my car's brakes. • potentially (*adverb*) Mountain climbing is a potentially dangerous activity.	• supposedly (*adverb*) The book is supposedly a true story about two scientists who were spies.

1. A _____ serious accident happened this morning. Fortunately, no one was hurt.

2. Hugo always attends class, _____ when he is working late.

3. The detective's report said the neighbor _____ saw the robber.

4. Is there a _____ benefit to taking daily vitamins?

5. The scientists _____ described their research.

Helen Keller

Without _____, Helen Keller was a great American. A childhood
                    6.

illness caused Helen to become blind and deaf. _____ for her
                                                        7.

teacher Annie Sullivan, no one thought Helen was able to live a full life. However, Annie

_____ taught Helen to develop her _____
        8.   **9.**

skills. Consequently, Helen became a source of inspiration for people. For someone who

_____ was not able to live a normal life, Helen Keller achieved
        10.

great success.

Which jobs need comprehensive training and knowledge?

Exercise 5 What Do You Think?

Read each question and write a brief answer. Explain your answers in complete sentences.

1. Which occupation potentially needs more comprehensive training and knowledge: a school principal or a restaurant owner? Be specific.

   _____

   _____

   _____

2. Which is more likely a source of potential problems: lack of preparation or unexpected circumstances?

   _____

   _____

   _____

3. Do you suppose that more exceptions to the law are made for celebrities than for average people? Why or why not?

   _____

   _____

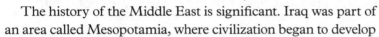

Exercise 6 Reading Connection

Read the following passage and answer the questions.

The Middle East

The Middle East is one of the most critical regions in the world. Why? The answer is oil. The Middle East contains enormous amounts of oil and natural gas. Much of the world relies on oil from the Middle East. Where exactly is the Middle East? What countries are included in the Middle East? What else is important to know about this region?

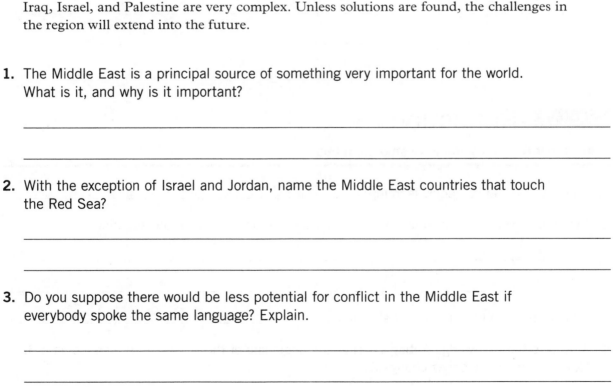

The Middle East is a large region where Europe, Africa, and Asia meet. It is a crossroads, made up of several countries. The climate is generally hot and dry. Three important rivers are located in the region. The Nile River is in Egypt, and the Tigris and Euphrates rivers are in Iraq. The largest country in the Middle East, Saudi Arabia, is mostly desert.

The history of the Middle East is significant. Iraq was part of an area called Mesopotamia, where civilization began to develop thousands of years ago. Iran was once called Persia. The Persian Empire was the largest empire in ancient history. In Egypt, the kings built the pyramids more than four thousand years ago.

Four of the world's major religions began in the Middle East. The religions are Islam, Christianity, Judaism, and Baha'i Faith. Although Arabic is the principal language, Farsi and Hebrew are also spoken in the Middle East.

Today the Middle East is the site of many conflicts. The problems in places like Iran, Iraq, Israel, and Palestine are very complex. Unless solutions are found, the challenges in the region will extend into the future.

1. The Middle East is a principal source of something very important for the world. What is it, and why is it important?

   _____

   _____

2. With the exception of Israel and Jordan, name the Middle East countries that touch the Red Sea?

   _____

   _____

3. Do you suppose there would be less potential for conflict in the Middle East if everybody spoke the same language? Explain.

   _____

   _____

alternative **comprehensive** presence
component extreme capacity **exception**
potential emerge besides extend design
feature extreme **source** component likely
prior prohibit restore principal **suppose**

New Word List

☐ comprehensive

☐ exception

☐ potential

☐ source

☐ suppose

Review Word List

☐ _____

☐ _____

☐ _____

☐ _____

☐ _____

Exercise 7 Writing Connection

Write a brief response to each question. Use words from this lesson or previous lessons in your answer. Write your answers in complete sentences.

It has been said that money is the source of all unhappiness. Do you agree? Explain your answer.

_____

_____

_____

_____

_____

What do you have the potential to do? Tell what it is and explain why you have this potential. How can you develop your potential?

_____

_____

_____

_____

_____

Exercise 8 Reflection

Think about the words you have studied in this lesson.

1. Which words did you enjoy learning? _____

2. Select one word and imagine where you will use the word. Explain the situation.

_____

_____

3. Which words do you still need help with? _____

4. Return to the Knowledge Rating Chart at the beginning of this lesson. Complete column 3. How have your responses changed?

alternative comprehensive besides **emerge**
source **extreme** capacity exception likely
potential besides extend **presence** design
prior feature extreme principal component
presence **prohibit** restore source suppose

Vocabulary Knowledge Rating Chart

How well do you know the words? Use the numbers to rate your knowledge of the vocabulary words. Follow the teacher's directions.

4 = I know the word. I know it well enough to teach it to someone else.
3 = The word is familiar. I think I know what it means.
2 = I have heard the word, but I'm not sure what it means.
1 = I don't know the word at all.

	My rating before instruction	I think the word means	My rating after instruction
emerge			
extreme			
presence			
prior			
prohibit			

Word Meaning Chart

Complete the chart. Follow the teacher's directions.

---

emerge *(verb)* /ih MURJ/

To **emerge** means to appear, come out, or become known.

EXAMPLES

The moon eventually _____ from behind the thick clouds.

Class Example: _____

My Example: When the basketball team **emerges** from the locker room, _____

---

extreme *(adjective)*) /ik STREEM/

Extreme means intense or to a great degree.

EXAMPLES

Space travel involves _____ dangers.

Class Example: _____

My Example: An **extreme** reaction to seeing a mouse is _____

---

presence *(noun)* /PREZ uhns/

The word **presence** tells that something or someone is in a place.

EXAMPLES

The envelope was opened in the _____ of the judge.

Class Example: _____

My Example: In the **presence** of strangers, children often feel _____

---

prior *(adjective)* /PRAHY er/

Prior means before or previous.

EXAMPLES

Higher-paying jobs usually require _____ experience.

Class Example: _____

My Example: **Prior** to coming to class today, _____

---

prohibit *(verb)* /proh HIB it/

To **prohibit** is to prevent or not allow something from happening.

EXAMPLES

Airline regulations _____ smoking on airplanes.

Class Example: _____

My Example: Something that **prohibits** me from sleeping is _____

Exercise 1   Use the Words

Complete each sentence. Write the correct form of the vocabulary word in the blank space.

1. Antarctica and the Sahara Desert are places to experience _____ temperatures.

2. Parents often _____ children from watching television unless their homework is complete.

3. New, relevant facts in the case _____ during the investigation.

4. How do city officials test for the _____ of bacteria in the water?

5. "I'm sorry," said Louise, "because of _____ plans, I cannot meet you for lunch today."

Exercise 2   Complete the Sentences

These sentences have been started for you. They are not complete. Complete them with your own words.

1. The presence of a police car on the road _____

_____

_____

2. At a prior time in my life, _____

_____

_____

3. When the firefighter emerged from the burning building, _____

_____

_____

4. The most extreme weather I have ever experienced was _____

_____

_____

5. If I were a principal, I would prohibit _____

_____

_____

_____

Words at Work

Circle the best answer to each multiple choice question below. Then write a brief response to the question that follows. Write your answers in complete sentences.

1. Initially, the copy store wanted to hire Duane for a manager's position. However, Duane will not get the job because new information has emerged. What new information emerged?

   (A) Duane did not sign his application.

   (B) Duane was not truthful about his prior experience.

   (C) Duane has a motorcycle license.

   When the new information emerged, why did it damage Duane's opportunity? _____

   _____

   _____

2. Company rules prohibit employees from accepting gifts from customers. Jo Ellen was given a $10 gift card for Coffee Corner. Is this a conflict for Jo Ellen?

   (A) No, because she likes coffee.

   (B) No, it is not a large amount.

   (C) Yes, it conflicts with company rules.

   What is something your work or school prohibits? _____

   _____

   _____

3. Jorge is writing an article for the school newspaper. The article is about the extreme behavior of some students after the football team won the championship. What is an example Jorge will relate in the article?

   (A) Students were singing and dancing.

   (B) Students threw things and broke windows.

   (C) Students cheered and threw confetti.

   Is extreme behavior an appropriate way to celebrate? _____

   _____

   _____

4. Terry's Toys intends to extend its presence beyond the city. How can it achieve this objective?

   (A) open a second location

   (B) get a new sign

   (C) analyze its inventory

   What is another way for a company to extend its presence? _____

   _____

   _____

Exercise 4 Word Families

Most words are part of a family of words. Study the word families on this page. Then fill in the missing words in the sentences below using the words from this lesson. Use the correct form of each word to complete the sentences.

---

emerge *(verb)*

- emerging *(adjective)*
  Emerging artists work hard to achieve success.

presence *(noun)*

- present *(adjective)*
  The winner of the raffle must be present to accept the prize.

extreme *(adjective)*

- extreme *(noun)*
  There are extremes in both liberal and conservative thinking.

- extremely *(adverb)*
  Pioneers faced extremely challenging conditions on their journeys.

prohibit *(part of speech)*

- prohibition *(noun)*
  Did the city's prohibition on smoking have a negative impact on businesses?

- prohibitive *(adjective)*
  Prohibitive housing costs mean many people cannot afford to live in some cities.

---

1. Although the movie was _____ long, we enjoyed the 3-D effects.

2. China is considered an _____ market for expensive consumer products.

3. Should there be a _____ on using disposable plastic shopping bags?

4. Rene was not _____ at choir practice last night.

5. Which of the teams will _____ as the state champions this year?

Extreme Sports

Bungee jumping and ice climbing are examples of something called extreme sports. These

sports have _____ in recent years and are _____
        6.   **7.**

popular with young athletes. Some people believe there should be a _____
                                                                        8.

on these sports because of the _____ of danger. However, a certain
                                      9.

amount of danger is _____ with any sport.
                        10.

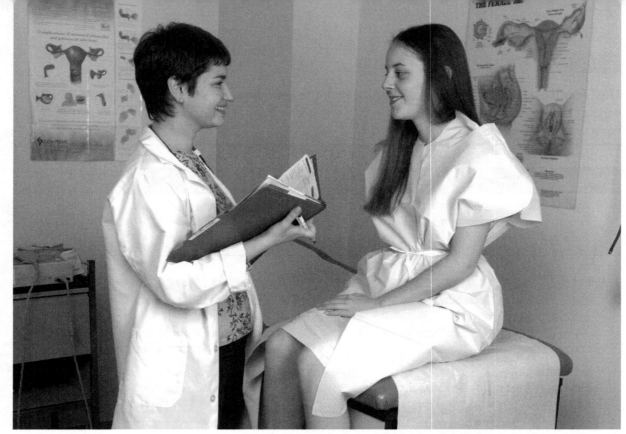

People often need medical treatment for a prior condition.

Exercise 5 What Do You Think?

Read each question and write a brief answer. Explain your answers in complete sentences.

1. Should a prior medical condition prohibit someone from getting health insurance?

   _____

   _____

   _____

2. Does the presence of parents or teachers prohibit children from expressing themselves?

   _____

   _____

   _____

3. If negative information emerged about a friend, would that change your prior feelings about the person?

   _____

   _____

   _____

Reading Connection

Read the following passage and answer the questions.

Anansi and the Turtle

Anansi the spider is an important character in West African folk stories. A folk story is designed to teach a lesson, or moral. What is the moral of this story?

Anansi liked yams, so one day he baked a few for dinner. As he sat down to eat, there was a knock at his door.

It was Turtle. "Hello, Anansi," said Turtle. "I have been walking all day, and I'm very hungry. Those baked yams smell quite good. Will you share your dinner with me?"

Anansi did not like the idea of sharing his yams. However, it was a custom in his country to share food with visitors. Therefore, he said, "Yes, please come in."

When Turtle sat down at the table, Anansi yelled out, "Turtle, it is not nice to come to the table with dirty hands!"

Turtle's hands were dirty. He got up and slowly walked down to the river to wash his hands. By the time he returned, Anansi had eaten all the yams. When Turtle left Anansi's house, he said to Anansi, "When you are in my country, come and share a meal with me."

One day, Anansi was in Turtle's country, and he remembered Turtle's invitation. It was near suppertime, so he went to Turtle's house in the river.

"I'm here to share a meal with you," said Anansi.

Turtle dived down into the river and called to Anansi. "Come down here. Everything is ready."

Anansi jumped into the river, but he could not dive deep into the water. He was too light, and he floated on the surface. He put some stones into the pockets of his jacket. Now he was able to dive deep and swim to Turtle's table.

Then Turtle said to him, "It is not polite to wear a jacket at the table in my country."

When Anansi took off his jacket, he floated up to the surface. From there all he could do was watch Turtle enjoy his meal.

1. Why is Anansi disturbed by the presence of Turtle at his door?

_____

_____

2. What prohibits Anansi from eating at Turtle's table?

_____

_____

3. Anansi tries to outsmart Turtle because he does not want to share his baked yams. What is the principal lesson, or moral, that emerges at the end of the story?

_____

_____

alternative comprehensive besides **emerge**
source **extreme** capacity exception likely
potential besides extend **presence** design
prior feature extreme principal component
presence **prohibit** restore source suppose

New Word List

☐ emerge

☐ extreme

☐ presence

☐ prior

☐ prohibit

Review Word List

☐ _____

☐ _____

☐ _____

☐ _____

☐ _____

Exercise 7 Writing Connection

Write a brief response to each question. Use words from this lesson or previous lessons in your answer. Write your answers in complete sentences.

Think of a prior experience that helped you emerge as a stronger or wiser person. Describe the experience and explain how it helped you emerge stronger or wiser.

_____

_____

_____

_____

_____

Imagine you are in the presence of your favorite movie, sports, or music celebrity. Who is the person? How do you feel about being in his or her presence? What would you like to tell or ask the person? Do your nerves prohibit you from speaking?

_____

_____

_____

_____

_____

Exercise 8 Reflection

Think about the words you have studied in this lesson.

1. Which words did you enjoy learning? _____

2. Select one word and imagine where you will use the word. Explain the situation.

_____

_____

3. Which words do you still need help with? _____

4. Return to the Knowledge Rating Chart at the beginning of this lesson. Complete column 3. How are your responses changed?

Activity 1 | Make Statements

Write five statements about the picture. Your statements can describe what you see or give an opinion. You can select a sentence starter from the chart to help you create interesting and different sentences. Use one or more of the vocabulary words you studied in this unit in each sentence. You may also use words from the previous unit. Underline each vocabulary word you use.

Examples: I think that <u>besides</u> having the <u>capacity</u> to kick the ball with both feet, a soccer player must be able to run fast.
In my opinion, the <u>presence</u> of many fans makes the game exciting.

Make an observation:	Give an opinion:
There is/There are…	I think…
I notice that…	In my opinion…
It seems that…	It's important/It's essential…

_____

_____

_____

_____

_____

_____

WORD BANK

ALTERNATIVE
BESIDES
CAPACITY
COMPONENT
COMPREHENSIVE
DESIGN
EMERGE
EXCEPTION
EXTEND
EXTREME
FEATURE
LIKELY
POTENTIAL
PRESENCE
PRINCIPAL
PRIOR
PROHIBIT
RESTORE
SOURCE
SUPPOSE

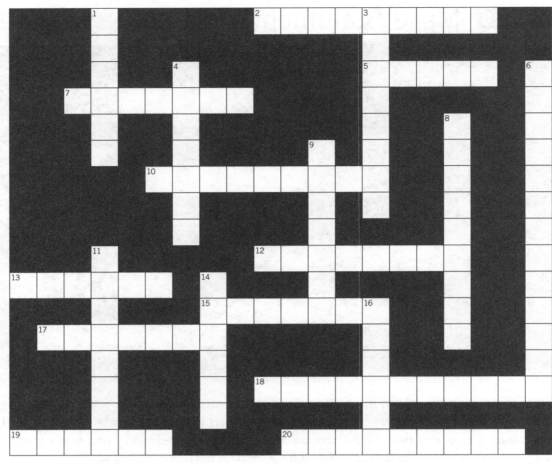

Activity 2 Puzzle

ACROSS

2. Scott's height is his _____ advantage.
5. More x-rays were needed _____ to the surgery.
7. Singing waiters are a unique _____ of the restaurant.
10. If one _____ is not connected, the stereo system will not work.
12. Why does the museum _____ people from taking pictures?
13. Citrus fruit is a good _____ of vitamin C.
15. With _____ difficulty, Ray finished the marathon.
17. Does Leo speak other languages _____ Russian?
18. Is there an _____ place to park?
19. Did Ms. Park _____ the deadline for registration?
20. Julia has the _____ to be a doctor.

DOWN

1. Is Toby _____ to get the job promotion he wants?
3. Jerry has the _____ to work under pressure.
4. Do you _____ it will rain tomorrow afternoon?
6. Bob's explanation was clear and _____.
8. With the _____ of Amy, everyone passed the test.
9. Mrs. Stein hopes the operation will _____ her vision.
11. The _____ of flowers makes a room brighter.
14. Sara likes to _____ jewelry to give as gifts.
16. We waited for the mayor to _____ from the meeting.

Activity 3 | Synonyms

Complete these sentences. Use the correct form of the vocabulary word that means the same as the word in parentheses.

Example: The solution to the conflict was comprehensive. _____Besides_____ (*also*), it pleased everyone.

1. The _____ (*other*) design was chosen because it cost less.

2. Why does the _____ (*possibility*) for extreme danger excite Jason?

3. Without exception, each soldier has the _____ (*ability*) to run 10 miles.

Activity 4 | Antonyms

Complete these sentences. Use the correct form of the vocabulary word that means the opposite of the word in parentheses.

Example: _____Prior_____ (*after*) to restoring the antique chair, Lisa kept it in the dusty basement.

1. Is it likely that the city will _____ (*shorten*) Main Street this summer?

2. The smoke was a _____ (*minor*) cause of the confusion in the building.

3. The store _____ (*allowed*) staff from using the computer components.

Activity 5 | Using the Vocabulary Words

Complete the paragraph with correct forms of the vocabulary words from this unit.

Marie Curie

In the early 20th century, Marie Curie _____ as the first major
1.
female scientist. She and her husband, Pierre, did _____ research.
2.
They explained the _____ of radiation in elements. They also discovered
3.
radium. Curie eventually learned that it had the _____ to treat cancer.
4.
_____ to Marie Curie, women were _____ from being part
5.   6.
of the scientific community. _____ being the first female professor at the
7.
University of Paris, she was the first woman to receive a Nobel Prize.

efficient

gain

state

contradiction

profit

particular

prominent

radical

apparent

function

exceed

monitor

cease

transform

version

status

overcome

sequence

transition

throughout

cease apparent function overcome profit
monitor prominent **efficient** contradiction
exceed **gain** overcome status particular
transform state profit monitor **radical**
version **transition** throughout sequence

Vocabulary Knowledge Rating Chart

How well do you know the words? Use the numbers to rate your knowledge of the vocabulary words. Follow the teacher's directions.

4 = I know the word. I know it well enough to teach it to someone else.
3 = The word is familiar. I think I know what it means.
2 = I have heard the word, but I'm not sure what it means.
1 = I don't know the word at all.

	My rating before instruction	I think the word means	My rating after instruction
cease			
efficient			
gain			
radical			
transition			

Word Meaning Chart

Complete the chart. Follow the teacher's directions.

cease *(verb)* /sees/ — To **cease** means to stop doing something.

EXAMPLES

Kelly _____ eating meat when she became a vegetarian.

Class Example: _____

My Example: The students **ceased** working when _____

efficient *(adjective)* /ih FISH uhnt/ — **Efficient** tells that a person or thing works well and does not waste anything.

EXAMPLES

My new dishwasher is _____. It uses less energy than my old one.

Class Example: _____

My Example: An **efficient** person _____

gain *(verb)* /gayn/ — To **gain** means to get or increase something.

EXAMPLES

America _____ its independence from Britain after the Revolutionary War.

Class Example: _____

My Example: I can **gain** experience by _____

radical *(adjective)* /RAD i kuhl/ — The word **radical** tells that something is extreme, new, or different.

EXAMPLES

Jeremy made a _____ decision to quit his job and leave immediately.

Class Example: _____

My Example: It would be a **radical** change if my class _____

transition *(noun)* /tran ZISH uhn/ — **Transition** is the process of changing from one condition or situation to another.

EXAMPLES

The _____ from cordless phones to cell phones happened quickly.

Class Example: _____

My Example: A person makes a **transition** when _____

Use the Words

Complete each sentence. Write the correct form of the vocabulary word in the blank space.

1. The new design for the cafeteria made _____ use of the space.

2. Do you agree with the principal's _____ strategy to extend the school day?

3. When people travel from the East Coast to the West Coast of the United States, they

   _____ time.

4. There is always a period of _____ when a new president takes office after an election.

5. After his shoulder injury, Hector _____ lifting weights.

Exercise 2 Complete the Sentences

These sentences have been started for you. They are not complete. Complete them with your own words.

1. People gain my trust when _____

   _____

   _____

2. The fans ceased to cheer when _____

   _____

   _____

3. A radical thing for me to do would be _____

   _____

   _____

4. It was easy for me to make a transition when _____

   _____

   _____

5. I make efficient use of my time by _____

   _____

   _____

Words at Work

Circle the best answer to each multiple choice question below. Then write a brief response to the question that follows. Write your answers in complete sentences.

1. The new owners decided to require all employees to wear uniforms starting next month. Why was this decision a radical change for the employees?

   (A) They do not like the uniforms.

   (B) They are used to wearing jeans and T-shirts.

   (C) They cannot find uniforms in their sizes.

   How does a radical change make people feel? _____

   _____

   _____

2. Cheryl is a popular supervisor. Besides being supportive, she also is very efficient. What is one example of Cheryl being efficient?

   (A) She gets answers to employees' questions quickly.

   (B) She takes coffee breaks with the employees.

   (C) She has many years of work experience.

   What is another example of being efficient at work? _____

   _____

   _____

3. G&S Electronics has three factories. One of the factories will cease production in three months. What is one impact this will have on employees?

   (A) All employees will have to change their break time.

   (B) Some employees will be transferred to the other factories.

   (C) Some employees will need child care.

   What will be another impact on employees when the factory ceases production? _____

   _____

   _____

4. The bus drivers signed a new contract last week. What is one thing they gained from the new contract?

   (A) longer bus routes

   (B) longer work days

   (C) longer break times

   What is another thing they gained from the new contract? _____

   _____

   _____

Word Families

Most words are part of a family of words. Study the word families on this page. Then fill in the missing words in the sentences below using the words from this lesson. Use the correct form of each word to complete the sentences.

---

cease *(verb)*

- **ceaseless** *(adjective)*
  The ceaseless rain of the preceding three days kept us indoors.

gain *(verb)*

- **gain** *(noun)*
  All the students made significant gains on the test.

transition *(noun)*

- **transitional** *(adjective)*
  There is always a transitional period when a student transfers to a new school.

efficient *(adjective)*

- **efficiently** *(adverb)*
  Ms. Evans ran the clinic efficiently, so patients did not have to wait long.

- **efficiency** *(noun)*
  Fuel efficiency is a principal feature of any new car.

radical *(adjective)*

- **radical** *(noun)*
  There are radicals in many political and religious groups.

- **radically** *(adverb)*
  The two groups are so radically different that they will never agree.

---

1. The speed and _____ of our paramedics have saved many lives.

2. Was the baby's weight _____ recorded on her chart?

3. Mother Teresa's _____ dedication to the extremely poor inspired the world.

4. We had to _____ revise the budget after we lost our funding for the project.

5. Unless you work _____, the house won't be clean before the guests arrive.

Retirement

Retirement is the time when older adults _____ working. Often it is not
$\underset{\text{6.}}{}$
an easy _____. Some people's lives change _____.
$\quad\quad\quad$ 7. $\quad\quad\quad\quad\quad\quad\quad\quad\quad\quad\quad\quad\quad$ 8.
In their prior jobs, many people were _____ workers who performed
$\quad\quad\quad\quad\quad\quad\quad\quad\quad\quad\quad\quad\quad$ 9.
their jobs _____. Now, they are not sure what to do and may require a
$\quad\quad\quad$ 10.
_____ period to adjust. Other people quickly _____
$\quad\quad\quad$ 11. $\quad\quad\quad\quad\quad\quad\quad\quad\quad\quad\quad\quad\quad\quad\quad\quad\quad$ 12.
new interests and become volunteers, students, or gardeners.

Efficiency and product knowledge are critical components of business success.

Exercise 5 What Do You Think?

Read each question and write a brief answer. Explain your answers in complete sentences.

1. Will a strategy to improve efficiency always gain new customers for a company?

_____

_____

_____

2. Is it easier or more difficult for children to gain independence if their parents cease worrying about them?

_____

_____

_____

3. Is it ever better to make a radical change instead of a slow transition?

_____

_____

_____

Reading Connection

Read the following passage and answer the questions.

The Republican Party

The Republican Party is one of the two principal political parties in the United States. The other party is the Democratic Party. The parties represent different points of view about the way the country should operate.

The Republican Party has a long history. Abraham Lincoln helped start the party in 1854. The country was still growing. The issue of slavery was causing great conflict. Lincoln and others formed the Republican Party to fight the extension of slavery into new states. In 1860, Lincoln was elected the first Republican president of the country.

The Republican Party is often referred to as the Grand Old Party, or GOP. The symbol of the GOP is an elephant. The elephant first appeared in a political cartoon. People started using it to represent the GOP.

Republicans believe that individuals have a better capacity to solve problems than government. Therefore, they favor a government that does not have a strong presence in people's lives. Republicans prefer lower taxes. They also prefer laws that support business and industry. This is considered a conservative point of view. It is a major difference between Republicans and Democrats.

People who are likely to support the Republican Party are farmers, business owners, and people who do not like high taxes.

Besides Lincoln, there are other important Republican presidents. Teddy Roosevelt helped create national parks. Dwight Eisenhower helped end segregation in public schools. Richard Nixon became the first president to resign. Other Republican presidents include Ronald Reagan and George W. Bush.

1. Abraham Lincoln and others who started the Republican Party wanted to cease slavery. Do you think that was a radical idea in 1854?

_____

_____

2. What do business owners believe they will gain if Republicans are running the government?

_____

_____

3. Republicans believe that individuals are more efficient than government at solving problems. In what ways is a government not always efficient? Try to use a specific example.

_____

_____

cease apparent function overcome profit
monitor prominent **efficient** contradiction
exceed **gain** overcome status particular
transform state profit monitor **radical**
version **transition** throughout sequence

New Word List

☐ cease

☐ efficient

☐ gain

☐ radical

☐ transition

Review Word List

☐ _____

☐ _____

☐ _____

☐ _____

☐ _____

Writing Connection

Write a brief response to each question. Use words from this lesson or previous lessons in your answer. Write your answers in complete sentences.

When young people make the transition from childhood to adolescence, they cease doing many things. What is one thing you ceased doing that is now a positive memory? Describe the activity and when you ceased doing it.

_____

_____

_____

_____

_____

Who is an efficient person that you know? Identify this person and tell how he or she is efficient. Give specific examples.

_____

_____

_____

_____

_____

Reflection

Think about the words you have studied in this lesson.

1. Which words did you enjoy learning? _____

2. Select one word and imagine where you will use the word. Explain the situation.

_____

_____

3. Which words do you still need help with? _____

4. Return to the Knowledge Rating Chart at the beginning of this lesson. Complete column 3. How have your responses changed?

cease apparent **function** overcome profit
monitor prominent efficient contradiction
exceed overcome gain **particular** status
transform **state** cease profit monitor radical
version transition sequence **throughout**

Vocabulary Knowledge Rating Chart

How well do you know the words? Use the numbers to rate your knowledge of the vocabulary words. Follow the teacher's directions.

4 = I know the word. I know it well enough to teach it to someone else.
3 = The word is familiar. I think I know what it means.
2 = I have heard the word, but I'm not sure what it means.
1 = I don't know the word at all.

	My rating before instruction	I think the word means	My rating after instruction
function			
monitor			
particular			
state			
throughout			

Word Meaning Chart

Complete the chart. Follow the teacher's directions.

function (noun) /FUHNGK shuhn/
A **function** is the job or purpose of someone or something.

EXAMPLES

The _____ of the lungs is breathing, or respiration.

Class Example: _____

My Example: The **function** of a test is _____

monitor (verb) /MON i ter/
To **monitor** is to watch something or someone for a specific purpose.

EXAMPLES

The doctor wants to _____ my blood pressure, so I get it checked once a month.

Class Example: _____

My Example: The cameras in a bank lobby **monitor** _____

particular (adjective) /per TIK yuh ler/
Particular means specific or certain.

EXAMPLES

Pay _____ attention to your spelling when you fill out the application.

Class Example: _____

My Example: A **particular** movie I recently enjoyed was _____

state (noun) /steyt/
A **state** is the condition of someone or something at a specific time.

EXAMPLES

What was the _____ of your car after the accident?

Class Example: _____

My Example: The **state** of the economy is _____ because _____

throughout (preposition or adverb) /throo OUT/
Throughout means everywhere or for the entire time.

EXAMPLES

Portuguese is spoken _____ Portugal and Brazil.

Class Example: _____

My Example: **Throughout** the holidays, _____

Use the Words

Complete each sentence. Write the correct form of the vocabulary word in the blank space.

1. The United Nations often _____ elections to make sure they are honest.

2. Members of a jury are prohibited from talking about a case _____ a trial.

3. What is the _____ of the vice president?

4. "The _____ of the company is considerably stronger this year than last," said the director.

5. The analysis of the complex problem was of _____ interest to the math teacher.

Exercise 2 **Complete the Sentences**

These sentences have been started for you. They are not complete. Complete them with your own words.

1. Henry was in a highly emotional state because _____

_____

_____

2. One particular experience that I will never forget is _____

_____

_____

3. Throughout my childhood _____

_____

_____

4. I monitor my spending by _____

_____

_____

5. The function of a library is _____

_____

_____

Words at Work

Circle the best answer to each multiple choice question below. Then write a brief response to the question that follows. Write your answers in complete sentences.

1. At Tony's Pizza, new servers are monitored closely for the first week. What is the reason the manager monitors new employees?

   (A) to make sure they like their jobs

   (B) to make sure they understand the menu

   (C) to make sure they enjoy the food

   What is another reason for the manager to monitor new employees? _____

   _____

   _____

2. Marilyn works at a shoe store. When a customer came in yesterday, she said to Marilyn, "I'm looking for a particular pair of running shoes, but I can't remember the brand name." Marilyn spent an hour showing the customer different shoes. However, the customer was not satisfied. Why?

   (A) She did not find the specific shoes she wanted.

   (B) She did not find her size.

   (C) She did not find the appropriate shoes.

   When have you looked for a particular thing while shopping? What was it? _____

   _____

   _____

3. Elite Electronics believes it is essential that its salespeople know the features and functions of the items they are selling. Therefore, they provide an extensive orientation for their new salespeople. What is likely to be part of the orientation?

   (A) an explanation of the purposes of its products

   (B) an explanation of how to develop new products

   (C) an explanation of how to design its products

   What do you think is the main function of the orientation? _____

   _____

4. Before the employees entered the building, their manager told them that there had been a burglary the night before. The police had already been there to get the relevant information. What was the state of their work site?

   (A) Someone broke in at 1:00 a.m.

   (B) There are 10 windows and 2 doors.

   (C) Everything was a mess.

   Give two particular details to describe the state of the workplace. _____

   _____

Word Families

Most words are part of a family of words. Study the word families on this page. Then fill in the missing words in the sentences below using the words from this lesson. Use the correct form of each word to complete the sentences.

---

function *(noun)*
• **function** *(verb)* *Mr. Johnston is our history teacher. He also functions as the baseball coach.* • **functional** *(adjective)* *The digital camera needs a battery to be functional.*

monitor *(verb)*
• **monitor** *(noun)* *The nurse closely watched the patient's heart monitor throughout the surgery.*

particular *(adjective)*
• **particularly** *(adverb)* *The service at Gina's Cafe is very good, and the bus staff is particularly efficient.*

state *(noun)*
• **state of mind** *(noun)* *My grandfather is 95 years old and his state of mind is excellent.*

1. The _____ of the filter in the furnace is to remove dust and dirt.

2. This article about the fare increase is _____ relevant to bus riders.

3. A watch is a very _____ piece of jewelry.

4. What was George's _____ when he heard the news?

5. The baby _____ lets Leticia hear her baby crying in another room.

State of Emergency

A mayor, governor, or president can declare a _____ of emergency.
6.

It is usually after a disaster, _____ a disaster that causes severe
7.

damage. Normal business _____ may cease temporarily.
8.

Throughout the damaged area, police or soldiers act as _____. They allow
9.

only _____ people, such as rescue workers, into the area.
10.

Is the function of exercise different for different people?

What Do You Think?

Read each question and write a brief answer. Explain your answers in complete sentences.

1. Is the function of exercise to improve a person's state of mind?

_____

_____

_____

2. Should an employer monitor employee phone calls throughout the work day?

_____

_____

_____

3. Should the state of the economy in Mexico or Canada be of particular concern to the average American?

_____

_____

_____

Reading Connection

Read the following passage and answer the questions.

Johannes Gutenberg

Imagine a world where it took several months to make one small book. A large book could require several years. Also imagine that one book could cost more than a person made in one year. That was the world of Johannes Gutenberg when he was born in Mainz, Germany, in 1398.

At that time, books were produced one by one. Some books were copied by hand. Others were printed from hand-carved wooden blocks. Each block represented one page or part of a page. Ink was put on the wooden block. To print a page, a piece of paper was pressed on to the block. The wooden blocks often broke apart because of repeated use.

Large books, like the Bible, that had many words took a long time to copy or print. Johannes Gutenberg changed that in 1450. He developed a method to print books with something called moveable type. In place of the wooden blocks, he used metal to make individual letters. The separate letters, or type, could be arranged to make different words. The type could be used again and again without breaking.

Gutenberg also invented a printing machine to use with his moveable type. This printing press allowed a person to put many sheets of paper through it quickly. In one day, the machine could produce 3,600 printed pages.

Gutenberg's invention reduced the time it took to make books. Many copies of one book could be made at the same time. Another outcome was that the cost of books decreased because they were faster and easier to make.

Gutenberg's invention emerged as one of the most significant events in modern history.

1. Describe the state of book printing before Johannes Gutenberg's invention.

_____

_____

_____

2. What was one of the particular functions of moveable type that made book printing easier?

_____

_____

_____

3. The popularity of books increased throughout Europe after Gutenberg's invention. What is one reason?

_____

_____

cease apparent **function** overcome profit
monitor prominent efficient contradiction
exceed overcome gain **particular** status
transform **state** cease profit monitor radical
version transition sequence **throughout**

New Word List

☐ function

☐ monitor

☐ particular

☐ state

☐ throughout

Review Word List

☐ _____

☐ _____

☐ _____

☐ _____

☐ _____

Exercise 7 # Writing Connection

Write a brief response to each question. Use words from this lesson or previous lessons in your answer. Write your answers in complete sentences.

Your friend Jerome lost his job and is feeling anxious. What recommendations can you make to help him improve his state of mind? What can he do to function better?

_____

_____

_____

_____

_____

Think of a particular interest you have had throughout your life. Describe this interest and how you developed it. Give specific examples.

_____

_____

_____

_____

Exercise 8 # Reflection

Think about the words you have studied in this lesson.

1. Which words did you enjoy learning? _____

2. Select one word and imagine where you will use the word. Explain the situation.

_____

_____

3. Which words do you still need help with? _____

4. Return to the Knowledge Rating Chart at the beginning of this lesson. Complete column 3. How have your responses changed?

cease **apparent** function overcome profit
gain prominent efficient **contradiction**
exceed overcome status gain particular
transform state cease **profit** monitor radical
version transition throughout **sequence**

Vocabulary Knowledge Rating Chart

How well do you know the words? Use the numbers to rate your knowledge of the vocabulary words. Follow the teacher's directions.

4 = I know the word. I know it well enough to teach it to someone else.
3 = The word is familiar. I think I know what it means.
2 = I have heard the word, but I'm not sure what it means.
1 = I don't know the word at all.

	My rating before instruction	I think the word means	My rating after instruction
apparent			
contradiction			
exceed			
profit			
sequence			

Word Meaning Chart

Complete the chart. Follow the teacher's directions.

apparent *(adjective)* /uh PAR uhnt/
Apparent tells that something is clear and easily noticed or that seems to be true.

EXAMPLES

It is _____ that the popular candidate will win the election.

Class Example: _____

My Example: The children's excitement was **apparent** when _____

contradiction *(noun)* /kon truh DIK shuhn/
Contradiction is the difference between two things that are opposed to each other.

EXAMPLES

One witness said the light was red. The other said it was green. There was a _____ between their statements.

Class Example: _____

My Example: It is a **contradiction** for a doctor to _____

exceed *(verb)* /ik SEED/
To **exceed** means to go over a set limit or to use more of something.

EXAMPLES

You can get a ticket if you _____ the speed limit.

Class Example: _____

My Example: The price of the computer **exceeded** my budget, so _____

profit *(verb)* /PROF it/
To **profit** means to benefit from something.

EXAMPLES

Young children _____ from having their parents read to them.

Class Example: _____

My Example: Students can **profit** from _____

sequence *(noun)* /SEE kwuhns/
Sequence means an order or a series of related events, actions, or things.

EXAMPLES

The trainer at the gym created a _____ of exercises for clients.

Class Example: _____

My Example: Something that has a **sequence** of events is _____

Exercise 1 Use the Words

Complete each sentence. Write the correct form of the vocabulary word in the blank space.

1. Do you think there is a _____ between the mayor's statement supporting public transportation and his vote against plans for a new subway system?

2. Shauna _____ from her volunteer experience at the downtown homeless shelter.

3. It helps to understand the _____ of events that led up to the conflict.

4. For no _____ reason, the coach ended the practice early.

5. Carlos _____ his parents' expectations when he won a scholarship to college.

Exercise 2 Complete the Sentences

These sentences have been started for you. They are not complete. Complete them with your own words.

1. Tanya's achievement exceeded the record at our school, so _____

_____

_____

2. Unless you follow the sequence of directions in the recipe, _____

_____

_____

3. I can profit from getting up early by _____

_____

_____

4. It is apparent that Reid is a hard worker because _____

_____

5. In contradiction to his prior statements about requiring uniforms, the boss _____

_____

_____

Exercise 3 Words at Work

Circle the best answer to each multiple choice question below. Then write a brief response to the question that follows. Write your answers in complete sentences.

1. A guest at Hotel Viva said, "This is my first time here. The service has exceeded my expectations." How does this guest feel?

   (A) satisfied   **(B)** irritated   **(C)** very pleased

   When service exceeds a customer's expectations, what is the customer likely to do? _____

   _____

2. Justin works 10-hour shifts. He has a schedule that follows an unusual sequence. He works 2 days and then has a day off. Then he works 2 days and has 2 days off. The sequence then repeats itself. If the sequence starts on Monday, what are his days off?

   (A) Wednesday, Friday,   **(B)** Wednesday, Saturday,   **(C)** Tuesday, Saturday, Sunday
   Saturday   Sunday

   Why does Justin like this sequence? How does he profit from it? _____

   _____

   _____

3. It is apparent to Ayshe that the new manager is having difficulty pronouncing her name. He is also mispronouncing several of her coworkers' names. What should Ayshe do?

   (A) speak to the manager   **(B)** laugh with her coworkers   **(C)** ignore his pronunciation
   privately to correct him   at the manager's
                                    mispronunciation

   How do you respond when someone makes an apparent mistake with your name or the

   names of your family or friends? _____

   _____

4. Saul works in a parking garage. He is very busy at particular times in the morning and in the evening. Throughout the afternoon, however, he usually has short periods of time when he is not busy. Saul is always prepared to profit from these times. How does he profit from them?

   (A) He drinks a can of soda.   **(B)** He listens to music.   **(C)** He studies and does
                                                                         his homework.

   How can you prepare to profit from delays and additional waiting time? _____

   _____

   _____

Word Families

Most words are part of a family of words. Study the word families on this page. Then fill in the missing words in the sentences below using the words from this lesson. Use the correct form of each word to complete the sentences.

---

apparent *(adjective)*

- apparently *(adverb)*
  Norma apparently spent a lot of time at the beach. She has a great tan.

contradiction *(noun)*

- contradict *(verb)*
  I asked for the manager because the salesclerk contradicted the newspaper ad.

- contradictory *(adjective)*
  After the flood, there were contradictory reports. We were not sure what to do.

profit *(verb)*

- profit *(noun)*
  We made a good profit from the garage sale and got rid of several things.

- non-profit *(noun)*
  The American Heart Association is a non-profit that depends on donations.

- profitable *(adjective)*
  Nick thought that computer training was a profitable way to spend the afternoon.

---

1. Science and religion are not always _____ points of view.

2. Sheila was _____ too tired to go to the gym after work yesterday.

3. How long will it take the restaurant to become _____?

4. Mrs. Nestor _____ herself when she said she was not home.

5. One Saturday a month, the coffee shop donates its _____ to a

   different _____ in the community.

Crime Investigations

Police first ask for a sequence of events to determine what happened and when.

They look for _____ in statements made by different people
                        6.

and _____ comments from the same person. When people lie,
           7.

they make _____ mistakes. The police want to know who will
              8.

_____ from the crime. Criminals think crime is _____.
      9.   **10.**

However, time in jail is not the _____ they imagined!
                                           11.

The Declaration of Independence promised freedom and liberty for all.

Exercise 5 What Do You Think?

Read each question and write a brief answer. Explain your answers in complete sentences.

1. Many of the men who signed the Declaration of Independence owned slaves. Do you think there was an apparent contradiction between the Declaration of Independence's promise of liberty for all and the presence of slavery?

   _____

   _____

   _____

2. Is there ever an apparent reason for a person to exceed the speed limit?

   _____

   _____

   _____

3. Is it an apparent conflict for a parent to profit from a child's success?

   _____

   _____

Reading Connection

Read the following passage and answer the questions.

The First Vaccine

Throughout history, diseases have been a major cause of death. People have looked for ways to prevent them. A vaccine is one way to prevent certain diseases. A vaccine introduces a mild form of a disease into the body. The body then produces special cells called antibodies to fight the disease. Consequently, the body is ready to defend itself against the more dangerous form of the disease.

Edward Jenner was a country doctor in England in the late 1700s. He discovered proof that a vaccine can prevent disease. Most of Dr. Jenner's patients were farmers who had cows. People who worked with cows often got a mild sickness called cowpox. Dr. Jenner noticed that these people never got smallpox, a very dangerous disease.

Dr. Jenner wanted to find a way to prevent smallpox. Therefore, he designed an experiment. He took a small amount of infected liquid from the skin sore of a person sick with cowpox. Then he put it into a cut on the arm of a little boy named James Phipps. He put a bandage on James's arm. Then everybody waited.

James got mildly sick. Six weeks later, Dr. Jenner repeated the procedure. This time, however, he used infected liquid from a person sick with smallpox. Fortunately, James did not get smallpox. Therefore, Dr. Jenner now had proof that a vaccine using cowpox could prevent smallpox.

The impact of Dr. Jenner's discovery was significant. Eventually, smallpox ceased to be a problem throughout the world. The last case was reported in 1977. Since the smallpox vaccine was discovered, scientists have developed vaccines for other major diseases. Today, vaccines are available for diseases like tuberculosis, polio, and swine flu.

1. What was the sequence of events in Dr. Jenner's experiment?

_____

_____

_____

2. How did the world profit from Dr. Jenner's experiment?

_____

_____

_____

3. How can a vaccine be considered a contradiction?

_____

_____

_____

cease **apparent** function overcome profit
gain prominent efficient **contradiction**
exceed overcome status gain particular
transform state cease **profit** monitor radical
version transition throughout **sequence**

New Word List

☐ apparent

☐ contradiction

☐ exceed

☐ profit

☐ sequence

Review Word List

☐ _____

☐ _____

☐ _____

☐ _____

☐ _____

Exercise 7 # Writing Connection

Write a brief response to each question. Use words from this lesson or previous lessons in your answer. Write your answers in complete sentences.

Think about an event or experience that exceeded your expectations. Describe it and tell why it exceeded your expectations.

_____

_____

_____

_____

_____

Reflect on the following quote: "Life is a contradiction at times—as are we." Do you agree with the quote? When have you experienced contradiction in your life or contradiction in another person? Have you experienced contradiction in yourself?

_____

_____

_____

_____

Exercise 8 # Reflection

Think about the words you have studied in this lesson.

1. Which words did you enjoy learning? _____

2. Select one word and imagine where you will use the word. Explain the situation.

_____

_____

3. Which words do you still need help with? _____

4. Return to the Knowledge Rating Chart at the beginning of this lesson. Complete column 3. How have your responses changed?

cease apparent profit function **overcome**
monitor **prominent** efficient contradiction
exceed overcome particular **status** monitor
transform state cease apparent radical
sequence throughout **version** transition gain

Vocabulary Knowledge Rating Chart

How well do you know the words? Use the numbers to rate your knowledge of the vocabulary words. Follow the teacher's directions.

4 = I know the word. I know it well enough to teach it to someone else.
3 = The word is familiar. I think I know what it means.
2 = I have heard the word, but I'm not sure what it means.
1 = I don't know the word at all.

	My rating before instruction	I think the word means	My rating after instruction
overcome			
prominent			
status			
transform			
version			

Word Meaning Chart

Complete the chart. Follow the teacher's directions.

overcome *(verb)* /oh ver KUHM/

To **overcome** is to fight against something and to succeed or win.

EXAMPLES

Lee had to _____ a serious knee injury to continue his running career.

Class Example: _____

My Example: One challenge single parents need to **overcome** is _____

prominent *(adjective)* /PROM uh nuhnt/

Prominent tells that something or someone is important, well-known, or large.

EXAMPLES

Soccer is one of the world's most _____ sports.

Class Example: _____

My Example: A **prominent** person in our community is _____

status *(noun)* /STEY tuhs/

Status means the social position or condition of a person or thing.

EXAMPLES

The principal asked the counselor, "What is the _____ of the graduation plan?"

Class Example: _____

My Example: I would describe my employment **status** as _____

transform *(verb)* /trans FAWRM/

To **transform** is to completely change a person or thing into something different.

EXAMPLES

The youth club _____ the yard behind the church into a community garden.

Class Example: _____

My Example: Computers have **transformed** the way we _____

version *(noun)* /VUR zhuhn/

Version means the form or description of something.

EXAMPLES

The drivers involved in the accident told different _____ of what happened.

Class Example: _____

My Example: I have heard more than one **version** of _____

Use the Words

Complete each sentence. Write the correct form of the vocabulary word in the blank space.

1. If you are not married, your marital _____ is single.

2. Arnelle _____ her nervousness and gave an excellent speech in class today.

3. Is it possible to _____ the health care system so everyone is included?

4. My computer is slow because it has an older _____ of the operating software.

5. Winston Churchill was one of the _____ leaders of World War II.

Exercise 2 Complete the Sentences

These sentences have been started for you. They are not complete. Complete them with your own words.

1. A prominent site in our city is _____

2. One thing Judy did to overcome her smoking habit was _____

3. I can check the status of _____

4. It is important to provide an accurate version of events when _____

5. My dream is to transform _____

Words at Work

Circle the best answer to each multiple choice question below. Then write a brief response to the question that follows. Write your answers in complete sentences.

1. Part of Ludmilla's job is to monitor sales and provide weekly status reports to her manager. What particular information is included in Ludmilla's status report?

   (A) the prior month's sales figures

   (B) the previous week's sales figures

   (C) next week's sales figures

   Why does the company want status reports? _____

   _____

   _____

2. Greg and Gloria want to transform their small restaurant into a friendlier, more fun café. What is something they can do to transform the space?

   (A) paint with bright colors

   (B) buy a bigger clock

   (C) keep the curtains closed

   What is another thing they could do to transform the restaurant? _____

   _____

   _____

3. Anderson has an entry-level job with the bank. However, he believes he has the potential to obtain a more prominent position. What position does Anderson believe he can achieve?

   (A) teller

   (B) supervisor

   (C) security guard

   What is a prominent position at your work or school? _____

   _____

   _____

4. Eliza had to overcome many challenges to finish school. What most likely helped her overcome the challenges?

   (A) extensive worrying

   (B) e-mailing her friends

   (C) persistence and self-confidence

   What else probably helped Eliza overcome her challenges? _____

   _____

   _____

Word Families

Most words are part of a family of words. Study the word families on this page. Then fill in the missing words in the sentences below using the words from this lesson. Use the correct form of each word to complete the sentences.

---

prominent *(adjective)*

- **prominently** *(adverb)*
  The American flag is prominently displayed on Memorial Day and Independence Day.

- **prominence** *(noun)*
  Rap music gained prominence in the 1980s.

status *(noun)*

- **status symbol** *(noun)*
  An expensive diamond necklace is considered a status symbol.

transform *(verb)*

- **transformation** *(noun)*
  A caterpillar goes through a transformation to become a butterfly.

---

1. Is gold considered a _____ in most cultures around the world?

2. The guest of honor was seated _____ at the head of the table.

3. Jacqueline Kennedy achieved a position of _____ among American first ladies.

4. The _____ of the classroom into a haunted house at Halloween surprised the students.

5. Although Mr. Vasquez is no longer the mayor, he is still a _____ member of the community.

6. Do not forget to check on the _____ of Jan's flight before you go to the airport to pick her up.

7. Automobiles _____ American society in the first half of the twentieth century.

Colonial Status Symbols

In Colonial America, the _____ of maps and globes increased as the
8.

colonies grew. Colonial gentlemen who were _____ and wealthy put
9.

them in their homes. They _____ placed maps and globes where
10.

visitors could easily see them. Maps and globes gained _____ as
11.

_____. Consequently, these objects were _____
12. 13.

from useful resources into symbols of the host's prominent status.

Students must overcome many challenges to reach graduation.

Exercise 5 What Do You Think?

Read each question and write a brief answer. Explain your answers in complete sentences.

1. Which will more likely transform a person's life: overcoming a fear or a physical challenge?

   _____

   _____

   _____

2. Is it easier for an average person or a prominent person to overcome a challenge?

   _____

   _____

   _____

3. Would you consider telling a different version of your life story to change or improve your social status or work status?

   _____

   _____

   _____

Reading Connection

Read the following passage and answer the questions.

Totem Poles

How would you tell the story of your family? Would you use words and pictures? Video? In parts of the Pacific Northwest region of North America, the native people use totem poles to tell their stories. This region includes the states of Washington and Alaska. It also includes British Columbia in Canada.

A totem pole is made from a tall cedar tree. Images of animals are carved into the wood. The animals are symbols, or totems. They represent particular experiences or qualities of the family, or clan. The carved pole is painted with traditional colors of red, blue-green, and black. A totem pole can be 50 feet high. The pole is placed at the entrance to the family's house. The carvings tell a story of the family's ancestors or experiences. It is not always easy to understand the story unless you are familiar with the symbols and the history of the family.

Initially, totem poles were small. They were approximately the size of a walking stick, or cane. However, in the 18th century, Europeans arrived in the Pacific Northwest. They brought strong tools made of metal. The native people used the better tools to carve bigger totem poles.

Particular animals appear on most totem poles. Each animal represents a spirit or special quality. Here are some of the most common animals.

- The Thunderbird, or "chief," is the most powerful of spirits.
- The Whale rules the underwater world.
- The Raven can transform itself into anything.
- The Bear has many human-like qualities and is very powerful.
- The Frog represents great fortune and wealth.

Totem poles are a unique feature of the native people of the Pacific Northwest coast.

1. How do Pacific Northwest native people transform cedar trees into totem poles?

_____

_____

2. Explain how a totem pole is a visual version of a family's story or experiences.

_____

_____

3. Which totem, or animal, has the most prominent status?

_____

_____

cease apparent profit function **overcome**
monitor **prominent** efficient contradiction
exceed overcome particular **status** monitor
transform state cease apparent radical
sequence throughout **version** transition gain

New Word List

☐ overcome

☐ prominent

☐ status

☐ transform

☐ version

Review Word List

☐ _____

☐ _____

☐ _____

☐ _____

☐ _____

Writing Connection

Write a brief response to each question. Use words from this lesson or previous lessons in your answer. Write your answers in complete sentences.

Think of a prominent person in the sports or entertainment field. Who is the person? Explain what the person has done to achieve prominent status.

_____

_____

_____

_____

_____

Significant inventions or discoveries, like the telephone or nuclear energy, can transform life for the average person. Name an achievement that has transformed life and explain how it changed the way people live. Give specific examples.

_____

_____

_____

_____

_____

Reflection

Think about the words you have studied in this lesson.

1. Which words did you enjoy learning? _____

2. Select one word and imagine where you will use the word. Explain the situation.

_____

_____

3. Which words do you still need help with? _____

4. Return to the Knowledge Rating Chart at the beginning of this lesson. Complete column 3. How have your responses changed?

Activity 1 · Write Statements and Questions

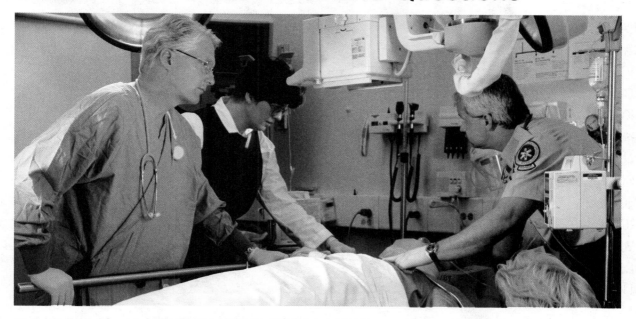

Write five statements or questions about the picture. You may select a sentence starter from the chart to help create interesting and different sentences. Use one or more of the vocabulary words you studied in this unit in each sentence. You may also use words from previous units. Underline each vocabulary word you use.

Examples: It seems that the medical staff is highly organized and <u>efficient</u>.
What is the <u>function</u> of the large machine above the patient?
Doctor, is there a <u>particular</u> <u>sequence</u> you follow in an emergency?

Make an observation:	Give an opinion:
There is/There are...	I think...
I notice that...	In my opinion...
It seems that...	It's important/It's essential...
Ask Questions:	
Who, What, When, Where, Why, How?	Do you think....?
	Is it important/Is it essential....?

_____

_____

_____

_____

_____

WORD BANK

APPARENT
CEASE
CONTRADICTION
EFFICIENT
EXCEED
FUNCTION
GAIN
MONITOR
OVERCOME
PARTICULAR
PROFIT
PROMINENT
RADICAL
SEQUENCE
STATE
STATUS
THROUGHOUT
TRANSFORM
TRANSITION
VERSION

Activity 2 Puzzle

ACROSS

6. Sam's plan is _____ but it may work.
9. Is the park open _____ the summer?
12. The movie _____ is not as good as the book.
16. An _____ cook does not waste any food.
17. When did women _____ the right to vote?
18. Do not _____ 6 pills in a 24-hour period.
19. What is Reyna's marital _____?
20. The photos were out of _____, so I was confused.

DOWN

1. Bert's _____ to college was easy.
2. Scientists _____ storms and potential hurricanes.
3. There is no _____ movie I want to see.
4. What is the _____ of the kidneys?
5. Did everyone _____ from the class?
7. There is a _____ between Cal's story and yours.
8. The bride's happiness was _____ to all.
10. Max wants to _____ his garage into an office.
11. The mayor is a _____ person in our city.
13. Our roads are in a terrible _____.
14. How did Alia _____ her fear of flying?
15. When did Josh _____ smoking?

Activity 3   Synonyms

Complete these sentences. Use the correct form of a vocabulary word that means the same as the word in parentheses.

Example: The employees did not _____profit_____ (*benefit*) from the changes.

1. Leo's improved physical _____ (*condition*) exceeded our expectations.

2. What is the _____ (*purpose*) of a college transition class?

3. You should do these _____ (*specific*) problems in sequence.

Activity 4   Antonyms

Complete these sentences. Use the correct form of a vocabulary word that means the opposite of the word or words in parentheses.

Example: Maya Angelou has _____prominent_____ (*unimportant*) status among poets.

1. Efficient workers _____ (*lose*) the respect of their managers.

2. Is it an _____ (*not clear*) contradiction for a nonprofit to make money?

3. Teachers _____ (*begin*) monitoring students' progress after graduation.

Activity 5   Using the Vocabulary Words

Complete the paragraph with the correct forms of the vocabulary words from this unit.

The Impact of Technology

    Technology has _____ our lives in many ways. The average
                    1.

person _____ from technology _____ an
       2.   **3.**

ordinary day. A _____ example is the cell phone. It made a
                4.

_____ difference in how we communicate. The impact of the
    5.

computer and the Internet is quite _____ as well. They allow us to
                                6.

_____ the _____ of our bank accounts from home.
  7.   **8.**

People have _____ doing many complex tasks. Computers perform these
                 9.

_____ more accurately. Consequently, jobs have been lost. It seems a
   10.

_____ that something designed to help us also has a negative impact.
   11.

Prefixes and Suffixes

Prefixes

A prefix is group of letters added to the beginning of a word. A prefix changes the meaning of the word.

The prefix **un-** means **not**.
likely   unlikely

The prefix **dis-** means **not**.
appear   disappear

The prefix **in-** means **not**.
appropriate   inappropriate
consistent   inconsistent
directly   indirectly
efficient   inefficient
sufficient   insufficient

The prefix **ir-** means **not**.
relevant   irrelevant

The prefix **mis-** means **wrongly**.
interpret   misinterpret
represent   misrepresent

The prefix **non-** means **not**.
profit   nonprofit

The prefix **re-** means **again**.
appear   reappear
apply   reapply

Suffixes

A suffix is a group of letters added to the end of a word. A suffix changes the part of speech.

The suffix **-able** changes a verb to an adjective.
obtain   obtainable
profit   profitable
recognize   recognizable

The suffixes **-al** and **-ial** change a noun to an adjective.
function   functional
sequence   sequential
transition   transitional

The suffixes **-ance** and **-ence** change a verb or an adjective to a noun.
appear   appearance
emerge   emergence
persistent   persistence
prominent   prominence
relevant   relevance
rely   reliance

Suffixes (*Continued*)

A suffix is a group of letters added to the end of a word. A suffix changes the part of speech.

The suffixes **-er, -or** an **-r** change a verb to a noun.

challenge	challenger
design	designer
develop	developer
interpret	interpreter
produce	producer
support	supporter

The suffix **-hood** changes an adjective to a noun.

likely	likelihood

The suffix **-ic** changes a noun to an adjective.

strategy	strategic
symbol	symbolic

The suffixes **-ion**, **-sion** and **-tion** change a verb to a noun.

apply	application
assume	assumption
contribute	contribution
determine	determination
express	expression
extend	extension
interpret	interpretation
modify	modification
omit	omission
produce	production
prohibit	prohibition
recognize	recognition
relate	relation
represent	representation
restore	restoration
transform	transformation

The suffix **-ity** changes an adjective to a noun.

complex	complexity
inevitable	inevitability

The suffix **-ism** changes a noun to another noun.

symbol	symbolism

The suffix **-ive** changes a noun to an adjective.

effect	effective

The suffix **-ize** changes a noun to a verb.

strategy	strategize
symbol	symbolize

The suffix **-less** changes a verb or a noun to an adjective.

cease	ceaseless
point	pointless

The suffix **-ment** changes a verb to a noun.

achieve	achievement
develop	development
involve	involvement

The suffix **-ness** changes an adjective to a noun.

appropriate	appropriateness

The suffix **-sis** changes a verb to a noun.

analyze	analysis
emphasize	emphasis

Glossary/Index

Use the glossary to locate and review the vocabulary words you have learned in this book. As you move ahead in your vocabulary study, the glossary can be a useful reference.

achieve *(v)* .... Lesson 5
to succeed by using effort or skill
  • achievement (n)

alternative *(adj)* .... Lesson 13
something that can be used in place of another thing
  • alternative (n)

although *(conj)* .... Lesson 2
shows contrast between two ideas in the same sentence
  • even though (conj) • though (conj)

analyze *(v)* .... Lesson 5
to examine something carefully to understand it
  • analysis (n)

apparent *(adj)* .... Lesson 19
something that is clear and easily noticed or that seems to be true
  • apparently (adv)

appear *(v)* .... Lesson 4
something or someone is seen
  • appearance (n)

apply *(v)* .... Lesson 6
to use knowledge or ability in a specific situation
  • application (n)

appropriate *(adj)* .... Lesson 1
something is right or acceptable
  • appropriately (adj)

approximately *(adv)* .... Lesson 8
a little more or less than an exact number or amount
  • approximate (adj)

assume *(v)* .... Lesson 11
to think or believe something is true without having proof
  • assumption (n)

average *(adj)* .... Lesson 12
possessing qualities that are common to most people or things
  • average (n)

basis *(n)* .... Lesson 2
the main reason or idea for doing or organizing something
  • based on (v) • basic (adj)

besides *(prep; adv)* .... Lesson 14
in addition to

capacity *(n)* .... Lesson 13
the ability to do, experience, or contain something
  • capable (adj) • capability (n)

cease *(v)* .... Lesson 17
to stop doing something
  • ceaseless (adj)

challenge *(v)* .... Lesson 4
to ask someone to test his or her ability to do something difficult
  • challenge (n) • challenging (adj)

circumstance *(n)* .... Lesson 3
the conditions or details concerning an event or situation

comment *(n)* .... Lesson 12
a spoken or written expression of an opinion or idea
  • comment (v)

complex *(adj)* .... Lesson 7
having many parts and being difficult to understand
  • complexity (n)

component *(n)* .... Lesson 14
one of several parts of something

comprehensive *(adj)*...................... Lesson 15
something that is complete and includes all
that is necessary
  • comprehensively (adv)

concept *(n)*............................. Lesson 7
an idea of what or how something is
  • conception (n)   • conceptualize (v)

conflict *(n)*............................. Lesson 9
a serious disagreement between people or
events
  • conflict (v)   • conflicting (adj)
  • conflict of interest (n)

consequence *(n)*....................... Lesson 2
the result, usually negative, of an action or
situation
  • consequently (adv)

considerable *(adj)*..................... Lesson 8
something that is large enough to be
important or noticed
  • considerably (adv)

consistent *(adj)*....................... Lesson 2
something or someone that continues to act
or be the same
  • consistently (adv)   • consistency (n)

content *(n)*............................. Lesson 1
the items, information, or ideas that are in
something
  • contain (v)   • table of contents (n)

contradiction *(n)*..................... Lesson 19
the difference between two things that are
opposed to each other
  • contradict (v)   • contradictory (adj)

contribute *(v)*......................... Lesson 9
to give help or to help something to happen
  • contribution (n)

critical *(adj)*.......................... Lesson 3
very important and serious
  • critically (adv)

design *(v)*............................. Lesson 14
to create or develop something
  • design (n)   • designer (n)

determine *(v)*.......................... Lesson 2
to figure out, solve, or decide something

develop *(v)*............................. Lesson 6
to create or to grow into something larger or
better
  • development (n)   • developed (adj)
  • developing (adj)

directly *(adv)*.......................... Lesson 7
having nothing or no one in between
  • direct (adv)   • direct (v)

duration *(n)*............................ Lesson 9
the length of time something continues

effect *(n)*.............................. Lesson 5
the change that results from an action by
someone or something
  • effective (adj)   • effectively (adv)

efficient *(adj)*......................... Lesson 17
a person or thing that works well and does
not waste anything
  • efficiently (adv)   • efficiency (n)

emerge *(v)*............................. Lesson 16
to appear, come out, or become known
  • emerging (adj)

emphasize *(v)*.......................... Lesson 4
to show that something is very important
  • emphasis (n)

eventually *(adv)*....................... Lesson 11
what happens in the end after a long time
  • eventual (adj)

exceed *(v)*............................. Lesson 19
to go over a set limit or to use more of
something

exception *(n)*.......................... Lesson 15
the person or thing that is not included or
does not follow a rule
  • except (prep; conj)

express *(v)* .... Lesson 3
to tell or show thoughts and feelings with
words, actions, or looks
- expression (n)\

extend *(v)* .... Lesson 13
to include, continue, reach, or make
something larger or stronger
- extension (n)

extensive *(adj)* .... Lesson 11
large in amount or degree
- extensively (adv)

extreme *(adj)* .... Lesson 16
intense or to a great degree
- extreme (n)   • extremely (adv)

feature *(n)* .... Lesson 14
an important or interesting part of something
- feature (v)

function *(n)* .... Lesson 18
the job or purpose of someone or something
- function (v)   • functional (adj)

gain *(v)* .... Lesson 17
to get or increase something
- gain (n)

impact *(n)* .... Lesson 11
the effect that an event or situation has on
someone or something
- impact (v)

inevitable *(adj)* .... Lesson 9
something that is certain to happen and
impossible to avoid
- inevitably (adv)

initial *(adj)* .... Lesson 6
at the beginning or first
- initially (adv)   • initiative (n)

intend *(v)* .... Lesson 12
to plan to do something

interpret *(v)* .... Lesson 12
to explain or decide the meaning of
something
- interpretation (n)

involve *(v)* .... Lesson 9
to include something or someone as a
necessary part
- involvement (n)   • involved (adj)

likely *(adj)* .... Lesson 13
something that will probably happen or is
almost certain
- likelihood (n)

modify *(v)* .... Lesson 8
to make small changes to improve something

monitor *(v)* .... Lesson 18
to watch something or someone for a specific
purpose
- monitor (n)

objective *(n)* .... Lesson 5
a goal or purpose

obtain *(v)* .... Lesson 11
to get something
- obtainable (adj)

omit *(v)* .... Lesson 8
to exclude or remove
- omission (n)

outcome *(n)* .... Lesson 4
the result of an action or event

overcome *(v)* .... Lesson 20
to fight against something and to succeed

particular *(adj)* .... Lesson 18
specific or certain
- particularly (adv)

persistent *(adj)* .... Lesson 5
not giving up or lasting a longer time than
usual
- persist (v)   • persistently (adv)
- persistence (n)

phase *(n)* .... Lesson 3
a step or stage in a process

point *(n)* .... Lesson 7
one idea, the most important idea, or the
purpose of something

potential *(n)*..................... Lesson 15
the possibility that something will develop or happen in the future
- potential (adj)
- potentially (adv)

preceding *(adj)*.................... Lesson 10
something that came before in time, order, or place
- precede (v)

presence *(n)*........................ Lesson 16
something or someone that is in a place
- present (adj)

principal *(adj)*...................... Lesson 14
something that is the most important
- principal (n)
- principally (adv)

prior *(adj)*.......................... Lesson 16
before or previous

produce *(v)*........................ Lesson 12
to grow or to make something
- producer (n)
- product (n)
- production (n)
- productive (adj)

profit *(v)*.......................... Lesson 19
to benefit from something
- profit (n)
- non-profit (n)
- profitable (adj)

prohibit *(v)*........................ Lesson 16
to prevent or not allow something from happening
- prohibition (n)
- prohibitive (adj)

prominent *(adj)*.................... Lesson 20
something or someone that is important, well-known, or large
- prominently (adv)
- prominence (n)

proof *(n)*.......................... Lesson 10
the information or evidence that shows something is true
- prove (v)

radical *(adj)*...................... Lesson 17
something that is extreme, new, or different
- radical (n)
- radically (adv)

recognize *(v)*...................... Lesson 1
to know someone or something from the past or to know that an idea is true or important
- recognition (n)
- recognizable (adj)

relate *(v)*.......................... Lesson 7
to make or show a connection to someone or something
- related (adj)
- relation (n)
- relationship (n)

relevant *(adj)*...................... Lesson 10
something that directly concerns the issue being considered
- relevance (n)

rely *(v)*............................ Lesson 3
to depend on or trust someone or something
- reliable (adj)
- reliance on (n)
- reliant on (adj)
- self-reliance (n)

represent *(v)*...................... Lesson 1
to stand for someone or something
- representative (n)
- representative (adj)

resource *(n)*....................... Lesson 8
something available to be used and that benefits the user
- resourceful (adj)

restore *(v)*........................ Lesson 13
to bring something back to its previous condition or situation
- restoration (n)

sequence *(n)*....................... Lesson 19
an order or series of related events, actions, or things

source *(n)*......................... Lesson 15
where something comes from

state *(n)*.......................... Lesson 18
the condition of someone or something at a specific time
- state of mind (n)

status *(n)*......................... Lesson 20
the social position or condition of a person or thing
- status symbol (n)

strategy *(n)*.............................. Lesson 6
a plan of action or a way to reach a goal
  • strategic (adj)

sufficient *(adj)*........................... Lesson 4
enough or adequate
  • sufficiently (adv)   • self-sufficient (adj)

support *(v)*.............................. Lesson 10
to provide help so that something can be
successful or survive
  • support (n)   • supporter (n)

suppose *(v)*............................. Lesson 15
to think or believe something is probably true
  • supposedly (adv)

symbol *(n)*.............................. Lesson 1
identifies an idea, feeling, or place
  • symbolic (adj)   • symbolize (v))

therefore *(adv)*................................. Lesson 10
consequently

throughout *(prep; adv)*...................... Lesson 18
everywhere or for the entire time

transform *(v)*................................. Lesson 20
to completely change a person or thing into
something different
  • transformation (n)

transition *(n)*................................. Lesson 17
the process of changing from one condition or
situation to another
  • transitional (adj)

unless *(conj)*... Lesson 6
except when or if not

version *(n)*................................. Lesson 20
the form or description of something

Image Credits

V(inset)The McGraw-Hill Companies, Inc./Jacques Cornell photographer, (t)Getty Images/ Blend Images; **3** Royalty-Free/CORBIS; **6** eddie linssen/Alamy; **11** Blend Images/Getty Images; **14** Purestock/PunchStock; **19** Royalty-Free/CORBIS; **22** Tim Boyle/Getty Images; **23** Glen Allison/Getty Images; **27** Royalty-Free/CORBIS; **30** Image Source/Alamy; **33** PhotoLink/Getty Images; **39** Somos Images/CORBIS; **42** Jupiterimages/Imagesource; **43** Robert Cornelius/ Getty Images; **47** Ingram Publishing/AGE Fotostock; **50** Royalty-Free/CORBIS; **51** Jack Moebes/ CORBIS; **55** moodboard/age fotostock; **58** Comstock Images/JupiterImages; **63** Royalty-Free/ CORBIS; **66** Jeremy Woodhouse/Getty Images; **67** Map Resources; **69** Yellow Dog Productions/ Getty Images; **75** The McGraw-Hill Companies Inc./Ken Cavanagh Photographer; **78** Ryan McVay/Getty Images; **83** CORBIS; **86** Hill Street Studios/Getty Images; **87** The McGraw-Hill Companies; **91** Photodisc/Getty Images; **94** The McGraw-Hill Companies, Inc./Andy Resek, photographer; **99** Somos/Veer/Getty Images; **102** Patrick Batchelder/Alamy; **105** PATRICK GARDIN/ASSOCIATED PRESS; **111** DBURKE/Alamy; **114** Royalty-Free/CORBIS; **115** Comstock Images/Getty Images; **119** Digital Vision/Getty Images; **122** Chuck Eckert/Alamy; **123** The McGraw-Hill Companies, Inc; **127** CORBIS; **130** (l)Jeff Greenberg/Alamy, (r)Image 100/CORBIS; **131** Map Resources; **135** Peter Casolino/Alamy; **138** Ken Karp for MMH; **141** Wei Zheng/Color China Photo/AP Images; **147** Craig Jones/Getty Images; **150** Jochen Sand/Getty Images; **151** Comstock Images/Getty Images; **155** Jamie Kripke/Getty Images; **158** Getty Images/Digital Vision; **163** Getty Images/Onoky; **166** Tom Grill/CORBIS; **171** Brand X Pictures/PunchStock; **174** Comstock Images/JupiterImages; **175** Image Source; **177** Dynamic Graphics/JupiterImages.